Uncover 3

Workbook with Digital Pack

Kathryn O'Dell

Shaftesbury Road, Cambridge CB2 8EA, United Kingdom

One Liberty Plaza, 20th Floor, New York, NY 10006, USA

477 Williamstown Road, Port Melbourne, VIC 3207, Australia

314–321, 3rd Floor, Plot 3, Splendor Forum, Jasola District Centre, New Delhi – 110025, India

103 Penang Road, #05–06/07, Visioncrest Commercial, Singapore 238467

Cambridge University Press & Assessment is a department of the University of Cambridge.

We share the University's mission to contribute to society through the pursuit of education, learning and research at the highest international levels of excellence.

www.cambridge.org
Information on this title: www.cambridge.org/9781107493452

First published 2015

40 39 38 37 36 35 34 33 32 31 30 29 28 27

Printed in Great Britain by CPI Group (UK) Ltd, Croydon CR0 4YY

A catalog record for this publication is available from the British Library.

ISBN 978-1-107-49345-2 Workbook with Digital Pack 3

Additional resources for this publication at www.cambridge.org/uncover

Cambridge University Press & Assessment has no responsibility for the persistence or accuracy of URLs for external or third-party internet websites referred to in this publication, and does not guarantee that any content on such websites is, or will remain, accurate or appropriate. Information regarding prices, travel timetables, and other factual information given in this work is correct at the time of first printing but Cambridge University Press & Assessment does not guarantee the accuracy of such information thereafter.

Art direction, book design, layout services, and photo research: QBS Learning

Table of Contents

1 Life on the Edge

VOCABULARY Extreme weather

1 Complete the sentences and the crossword.

```
          ¹
     ²w  i  n  d  s
   ³
 ⁴ ⁵
⁶
   ⁷
```

ACROSS

2. We didn't go for a boat ride because of high
   ____winds____.

4. There was a lot of _____ and lightning
   during the storm.

6. We couldn't see the road very well because of
   the _____. It was very thick.

7. It started to _____ during the storm.
   We were afraid the windows might break from
   the ice.

DOWN

1. I didn't have school today because of the
   _____.

3. It was over 35°C during the _____
   wave.

5. The game was canceled because of
   _____ rain.

2 Complete the weather report with words and
phrases from Exercise 1.

Worldwide Weather

There is a ¹ ____blizzard____ in Anchorage, Alaska,
today. Expect 25 to 50 centimeters of snow by the end of
the day. ² _____ of 80 kilometers per hour
are blowing the snow around.

³ _____ is coming down quickly in several
cities in southern Germany. Falling ice can damage cars
and hurt people.

Today in Mexico City there is ⁴ _____
falling at about 3 centimeters per hour. Right now, it's quiet,
but expect ⁵ _____ at night.

The Golden Gate Bridge is closed in San Francisco because
of ⁶ _____. Drivers can't see very far in
front of them. Be careful on the roads.

There is a ⁷ _____ in Dubai with
temperatures over 40°C.

3 What kinds of extreme weather do you think can
happen in these places?

1.
   high winds, _____

2. _____

3. _____

1 Look at Eva's weekend schedule. Complete the sentences about her routine with the simple present forms of the verbs.

Friday	Saturday	Sunday
go to class	work at food court	visit grandparents
study with Kyle at library	hang out with friends	make lunch with grandma

1. Eva _____goes_____ to class on Fridays.
   She _____doesn't go_____ to class on Saturdays and Sundays.

2. Eva and Kyle _____ at Eva's house. They _____ at the library.

3. Eva _____ at the food court on Saturdays. She _____ at the bike shop.

4. Eva and her friends _____ after work.

5. Eva _____ her grandparents on Sundays.

6. Eva and her grandma _____ lunch. Her grandpa _____ lunch.

2 Put the words in the correct order to make sentences. Change the verbs to the present continuous.

1. right / the snow / now / melt

   The snow is melting right now.

2. fly / Jake / to Alaska

   _____

3. in the park / play / they / basketball

   _____

4. my / I / skateboard / not ride

   _____

5. vacation / plan / a / we

   _____

6. and Tara / coats / not wear / Ed

   _____

3 Check (✓) if the activities are routines or happening right now.

	Routine	Right now
1. I'm driving in a blizzard.		✓
2. Dennis goes to the beach with his friends.		
3. Sarah drives to class.		
4. You aren't visiting your cousins.		
5. We are going to the beach with our friends.		
6. Mark and Penny visit their grandparents.		

4 Complete the conversation with the simple present or present continuous forms of the verbs.

Tina: Hi, Leo. What are you doing these days?

Leo: I [1]____am taking____ (take) a class at the community center, and I [2]_____ (play) on a new soccer team. I [3]_____ (be) really busy.

Tina: What class?

Leo: It [4]_____ (be) a meteorology class. You know, a class about weather.

Tina: I see. What are you studying?

Leo: Well, right now, we [5]_____ (learn) about weather changes around the world.

Tina: That sounds interesting.

Leo: Yeah. The weather [6]_____ (change) a lot these days. I [7]_____ (read) a chapter about extreme weather right now.

Tina: Speaking of weather, I have to go! It [8]_____ (start) to rain.

Leo: Oh, no. I guess I [9]_____ (not go) to my soccer game now. We [10]_____ (play) at the park every Tuesday, but we [11]_____ (not go) when it rains!

VOCABULARY Basic needs

1 Label the pictures with the correct words.

clothes	health care
communication	a home
education	money
entertainment	transportation
✓ food and drink	

1. _____*food and drink*_____   2. _____

3. _____   4. _____

5. _____   6. _____

7. _____   8. _____

9. _____

2 Complete the sentence with the words and phrases from Exercise 1.

1. My cousin wants to buy _____*a home*_____ in our neighborhood, but he doesn't have enough _____ yet.

2. There are many _____ options in this city – buses, trains, and subways.

3. I'm getting a good _____ at Clinton High School.

4. I need to buy some new _____ for school.

5. Texting is a more popular form of _____ than talking on the phone for teens.

6. Do you go to the movies for _____?

7. You can get _____ at the food court in the mall.

8. My parents have good _____. Their doctor is excellent.

3 Answer the questions with your own information.

1. What do you usually do for entertainment?

   *I usually watch movies on my computer.*

   _____

2. How much money do you spend every week?

   _____

   _____

3. What form of transportation do you use to get to school?

   _____

   _____

4. What is the main form of communication you use with your friends?

   _____

   _____

5. What kind of clothes do you like to wear?

   _____

   _____

**Past tense review –
simple past and past continuous**

1 Write sentences with the simple past.

1. Larry / get / home late last night
   Larry got home late last night.

2. We / not go / to the concert
   _____

3. I / send / Jen three text messages
   _____

4. They / ride / their skateboards to school
   _____

5. You / not call / last night
   _____

6. Sandra / wear / jeans to school
   _____

7. I / not be / at school yesterday
   _____

8. My cousin / arrive / from Argentina last night
   _____

**2 Complete the sentences with the past continuous
forms of the verbs.**

1. Laura _____*was studying*_____ (study) during
   the blizzard.

2. Vic and Dan _____ (ride) the
   bus together.

3. We _____ (not walk) outside
   when it started to hail.

4. I _____ (not wear) a coat when
   it got cold.

5. You _____ (shop) when
   I called you.

6. Frank _____ (wear) a helmet
   when he fell off his bike.

**3 Complete the sentences with the simple past or
past continuous forms of the verbs.**

1. I _____*didn't watch*_____ (not watch) the news
   last night. I was too busy!

2. Torrey _____ (see) the tornado
   before it hit the town.

3. I put on a hat, but the wind _____
   (blow) it off my head.

4. Jess _____ (not wear) a raincoat
   when the rain came, so she got really wet.

5. Sam _____ (listen) to the radio
   when he heard the weather report.

6. Reggie _____ (not be) afraid of
   storms until he experienced high winds.

4 Correct the sentences and questions.

                 used
1. Marcos ~~use~~ to play in the snow.

2. We use drive to California every summer.

3. Rita not used to take the bus to school.

4. Did you used to camp in the mountains?

5. I used to bought new clothes at the mall.

6. Jack and Paul use to watch TV on Saturday
   mornings.

**5 Complete the text with the simple past, past
continuous, or *used to*.**

On the Edge

Tonya Harris lives on the edge – on the edge of a
mountain! One time, she and her younger brother
[1] ___*were playing*___ (play) soccer outside
when her brother [2] _____
(kick) the ball off the mountain. He
[3] _____ (chase) the ball when Tonya
[4] _____ (scream). She [5] _____
(stop) him from going over the edge of the mountain. Now that
her brother is older, she doesn't worry about him, but she
[6] _____ (worry) about him all the time!
Tonya's school is at the bottom of the mountain. When she
was young, she [7] _____ (take) the bus to
school, but now she rides her bike. Yesterday, she
[8] _____ (ride) her bike when she
[9] _____ (fall). She [10] _____
(break) her arm. Her parents [11] _____ (drive)
to work when they [12] _____ (see) her. They
[13] _____ (take) her to the doctor right away.
Tonya [14] _____ (not go) to school yesterday.
This morning, Tonya [15] _____ (go) back to
school. While her friends [16] _____ (wait) for
class to start, they [17] _____ (write) their names
on her cast. Tonya likes her life on the edge of the mountain, but
she's going to be more careful!

1. Circle the correct answers.

1. **A:** This weather is crazy, _____?
   B: Yeah. It's an incredible blizzard.
   (a. don't you think)   b. I disagree

2. **A:** Do you think it's going to snow more?
   B: _____. I think the blizzard is over.
   a. I disagree   b. I don't think so

3. **A:** I hate winter weather.
   B: _____. I love the snow!
   a. See what I mean   b. I disagree

4. **A:** The snow is so high!
   B: _____? I told you it was 30 centimeters!
   a. See what I mean   b. I don't think so

5. **A:** I can't wait for spring. _____?
   B: Actually, I like the winter.
   a. Don't you agree   b. See what I mean

2 Circle the correct phrases.

Tim:	Can you believe this blizzard? It's the biggest one so far this year, [1]**I don't think so / don't you think**?
Donna:	Yes, I think you're right. There's at least 30 centimeters of snow on the ground! It'd be better to live somewhere warm. [2]**Don't you agree / I disagree**?
Tim:	[3]**See what I mean / I don't think so.** I really like the cold weather.
Donna:	Really? I prefer a warmer place. There's so much more to do in warm weather!
Tim:	[4]**I disagree / Don't you agree!** I do a lot in the winter. There are so many winter activities here – like snowboarding and skiing.
Donna:	We did have fun on the ski trip last weekend.
Tim:	[5]**I don't think so / See what I mean?** Winter is great.
Donna:	Yeah, I guess so. But this blizzard is terrible! It's too cold to ski or snowboard.
Tim:	That's true.

READING TO WRITE

1 Number the parts of a persuasive email in order from 1–3.

_____ Explain why you think your readers should do what you're suggesting.

_____ State your position again in a different way.

_____ State your position on a topic.

2 Circle the correct words.

```
○○○
🗎 🗁 ◁ 📎 🗑
      To  martin@net.cup.org
    From  lydia@net.cup.org
 Subject  Cuernavaca is the best!
```

Hi Martin,

I'm living in Cuernavaca in Mexico now. I love it. I think it's the best city in Mexico!

¹**First of all** / **Second**, it's like spring all year. ²**The best part** / **For example**, there are a lot of flowers and plants everywhere – all year long.

³**For example** / **Second**, there's a lot to do and see in Cuernavaca. ⁴**For instance** / **First of all**, there are historic buildings, carnivals, and a lot of markets.

⁵**The best part** / **For example** is the people. There are many places to meet friends. I met two new friends at the skate park yesterday!

Cuernavaca really is a great place to live. I hope you can visit me this year.

Your cousin,

Lydia

3 Match the sentences. Then write them in the correct places in the email.

1. The best part is all of the places to eat. _____

2. First of all, there are many things to do outside. _____

3. Second, there are many things to do inside. _____

a. For example, you can go to sports events and parks.

b. For instance, there are many museums in Chicago.

c. Chicago has food from all over the world!

```
○○○
🗎 🗁 ◁ 📎 🗑
      To  evelyn@net.cup.org
    From  talia@net.cup.org
 Subject  Come to Chicago!
```

Hi Evelyn,

I want you to come visit me in Chicago on your school break! Chicago is one of the best cities to visit.

_____

_____

_____

_____

_____

_____

So please come visit me. We'll have lots of fun!

Your friend,

Talia

2 First Things First!

1 **Put the words in the correct order to make phrases about priorities.**

1. out / working

   working out

2. out / weekend / on / staying / the / late

   _____

3. with / hanging / friends / out

   _____

4. clothes / for / shopping

   _____

5. the / helping / house / around

   _____

6. something / doing / creative

   _____

7. for / time / having / yourself

   _____

8. friends / online / chatting / with

   _____

9. enough / sleep / getting

   _____

2 **What are the people doing? Write sentences using eight of the phrases from Exercise 1.**

1. Carol is communicating with Jim and Vicky on her computer.

   She's chatting with friends online.

2. Brad went to bed at 9:00 p.m. last night. It's 8:00 a.m., and he's still in bed.

   _____

3. Jenny and Mark are exercising at the gym.

   _____

4. Mandy is looking at T-shirts and jeans.

   _____

5. Trent and Sue are cleaning the kitchen and washing clothes.

   _____

6. It's Saturday at 11:00 p.m. Wendy is at a concert.

   _____

7. Carlos is talking at a café with Luke, Dana, and Cindy.

   _____

8. Luisa is painting a picture.

   _____

3 **Answer the questions with your own information.**

1. What do you do when you have time for yourself?

   When I have time for myself, I read in the park.

   _____

2. How late do you stay out on the weekends?

   _____

   _____

3. Where do you hang out with friends? What do you do?

   _____

   _____

4. Do you help around the house? What do you do?

   _____

   _____

5. Do you like shopping for clothes? Where do you go?

   _____

   _____

GRAMMAR · have to/don't have to; must

1 Look at Matt and Carrie's To Do list and write sentences about their chores. ✓ = *have to*, ✗ = *not have to*.

To Do Weekend chores and activities		
Matt	**Carrie**	**Both**
shop for clothes ✓	work out ✗	help around the house ✓
fix the computer ✓	practice the piano ✓	work in the yard ✗
go to soccer practice ✗	take the dog for a walk ✓	do homework ✓

1. *Matt has to shop for clothes.*
2. _____
3. _____
4. _____
5. _____
6. _____
7. _____
8. _____
9. _____

2 Write sentences about the skate park rules with *must* and *must not*.

Do . . .	Don't . . .
• wear a helmet • take turns on the ramps • throw away trash	• bring food or drink into the skate area • use the park after 9:00 p.m. • ride bikes on the ramps

1. *You must wear a helmet.*
2. _____
3. _____
4. _____
5. _____
6. _____

3 Write two sentences for each picture with the words from the box and the correct form of (*not*) *have to* or *must* (*not*).

> you / turn off / your phone
> she / call / her mother now
> you / use / your phone
> she / call / her mother later

1. _____
2. _____

3. _____
4. _____

4 Write sentences about your chores with (*not*) *have to*.

> **Have to**
> 1. *I have to wash the dishes.*
> 2. _____
> 3. _____
> **Don't have to**
> 4. _____
> 5. _____
> 6. _____

5 Write sentences about rules for a library with *must* (*not*).

> **Dos**
> 1. _____
> 2. _____
> **Don'ts**
> 3. *You must not run in the library.*
> 4. _____

VOCABULARY Emotions

1 Find six more words for emotions.

S	H	I	O	H	P	R	O	F	G	W	U	M	K	P
T	B	S	P	Z	J	X	G	V	R	Q	I	A	Q	N
R	R	L	R	N	B	A	A	W	F	U	L	W	C	Z
E	M	I	O	M	D	D	Y	B	N	A	T	O	E	F
S	L	U	U	I	G	Z	K	P	D	Y	N	N	X	V
S	Z	U	D	U	N	A	W	E	P	G	E	D	H	L
E	M	B	A	R	R	A	S	S	E	D	R	E	A	B
D	I	S	U	R	H	I	Q	U	R	B	A	R	U	D
O	F	Z	S	C	K	R	J	G	E	F	P	F	S	P
U	E	T	E	R	R	I	F	I	E	D	K	U	T	M
T	H	W	N	N	X	H	T	S	T	M	H	L	E	O
G	V	K	A	S	L	S	T	P	R	H	X	E	D	T

2 Complete the sentences with the correct words.

awful
embarrassed
exhausted
proud
✓ stressed out
terrified
wonderful

I have so much to do this week. I'm really
¹ _____stressed out_____ ! First of all, I have to
give a speech in my class on Friday. I'm
² _____ because I really don't
like speaking in front of people. I worked on
the speech for hours last night, and today I'm
³ _____ . Last time I gave a
speech, I was so ⁴ _____
because I forgot what to say. It was
⁵ _____ ! But I'm going to
practice a lot this time. I hope it's going to be
⁶ _____ . I want to make my
parents ⁷ _____ .

3 How do you think the people feel in these situations? Use some of the words from Exercise 2. Sometimes more than one answer is possible.

1. John forgot his teacher's name. ___*embarrassed*___

2. Linda is scared of spiders, and there is a huge one under her bed. _____

3. Abby has three tests tomorrow, and she has to take care of her younger brothers tonight. _____

4. Oliver's sister scored three goals in a soccer game. _____

5. Danny didn't get enough sleep last night. _____

4 How do you feel in these situations? Use words from Exercise 2.

1. You did well on a test. _____

2. You're riding a roller coaster. _____

3. You have to give a speech. _____

4. Your friend won an award. _____

GRAMMAR Modals of obligation – *should, ought to, had better*

1 Complete the advice with *should* (*not*) and the verbs.

Mike G My friends are going sky diving tomorrow, but I don't want to go. I'm terrified! What should I do?

Sara Li You ¹_____ (be) embarrassed. It's OK if you don't want to go.

Dave I agree. You ²_____ (tell) your friends you don't want to go.

Paula S I disagree. You ³_____ (try) it. It might be really fun!

Steven You ⁴_____ (go) with them on the plane. It will be fun. But, if you get scared, you ⁵_____ (jump). You ⁶_____ (do) anything that you don't want to do. You can decide when you get there.

2 Look at the pictures and complete the sentences with *ought (not) to* and the correct verbs.

No Parking

1. We ___ought not to park___ here.

Turn your cell phones off

2. You _____ your cell phone off.

You can't take big bags on the plane

3. I _____ this bag on the plane. I'll have to check it.

Please be quiet

4. You _____ quiet in the library.

Don't sit on the grass

5. They _____ on the grass in the park.

3 Write sentences with *had better (not)*. ✓ = yes, ✗ = no.

1 Terry / hang out / with his friends tonight / ✗

Terry had better not hang out with his
friends tonight.

2. Josh and Mia / shop / for clothes before school starts / ✓

_____

3. We / get / home on time / ✓

_____

4. You / chat / online very long / ✗

_____

5. Serena / help / around the house / ✓

_____

6. I / get / too stressed out / ✗

_____

It's + adjective + infinitive

4 Correct the sentences.

    It's
1. ~~It~~ easy to be proud of your friends.

2. It's no difficult to ride a bike.

3. You shouldn't to stay out late.

4. It's important have time for yourself.

5. It fun not to shop for clothes.

6. You ought call the police about the robbery.

7. It's important is quiet in the library.

8. You had better to get enough sleep.

5 Read the sentences. Then write sentences with similar meanings with the modals.

1. It's a good idea for John to work out. (should)

    John should work out.

2. My cousin needs to call me. (had better)

_____

3. You can't drive on that side of the road. (ought not to)

_____

4. We can't stay out too late. (had better not)

_____

5. It's required that I buy a ticket before I get on the bus. (ought to)

_____

6. It's a bad idea for Lori to chat online with her friends for hours. (shouldn't)

_____

1 Put the words in order to make sentences.

1. show / let / you / me

   Let me show you.

2. at / very / that / I'm / like / not / good / things

   _____

3. if / you / like / I'll / give / a hand / you

   _____

4. really / simple / it's / pretty

   _____

5. not / how / it / I'm / sure / to do

   _____

2 Complete the conversation with the sentences from Exercise 1.

Sam:	Hey, Dee.
Dee:	Hi, Sam. It looks like you're having problems with your phone. ¹ *I'll give you a hand if you like.*
Sam:	That'd be great. I need to get my email on my phone, but ² _____ Do you know how?
Dee:	Yeah, I do. I just did it with my new phone last week. ³ _____
Sam:	Well, you might think it's easy, but ⁴ _____ I'm really terrible with technology.
Dee:	It's really not difficult to do. ⁵ _____ You'll see.
Sam:	OK. Thanks.
Dee:	So, first, go to "Settings" and click on "Email." Then click on "Add account" and enter your email address.
Sam:	Wow. That *was* easy. Thanks.

READING TO WRITE

1 Complete Lucas's blog post with *a few, a little, too many,* or *too much*.

Last month, I was really stressed out. I was involved in
¹ _____*too many*_____ activities. I was taking three
classes, working part-time at the mall, working out at
the gym, and playing on a soccer team. I was doing
² _____ ! I only had ³ _____
time to hang out with my friends. At the end of the week,
I was exhausted, and I really missed my friends.

I made some changes in my lifestyle. I made sure that I had
⁴ _____ minutes for myself each day.
Every morning, I read before breakfast, and at night, I took
⁵ _____ time to play video games. I
also made sure I was getting enough sleep. Then I started
doing some of my needed activities with friends. I started
working out with ⁶ _____ friends and
studying for my classes with my best friend. I still have
⁷ _____ to do, but at least I'm seeing my
friends more!

2 Read Lucas's blog post again. Answer the questions.

1. What was Lucas's problem?

   _____

2. What four things caused his problem?

   _____

   _____

   _____

   _____

3. What three steps did Lucas take to solve his problem?

   _____

   _____

   _____

3 Read Lucas's blog post again. Check (✓) the advice he would give other people.

If you are involved in too many activities, . . .

☑ you have to have time for yourself.

❏ you shouldn't work out.

❏ you should try to do some of your activities with other people.

❏ you can study with friends.

❏ you shouldn't study so much.

❏ you had better quit your job.

❏ you should sleep less to make time to get all of your work done.

❏ you ought to get enough sleep.

4 Complete the end of Lucas's blog post with the phrases you checked in Exercise 3.

If you're like me and are involved in too many activities,
I have some advice for you. ¹ *You have to have*
time for yourself. For example, read a book, ride
your bike, or play video games for a few minutes.
² _____

   _____

For instance, you can work out with people in your family, or
³ _____

   _____

⁴ _____

   _____ In fact,
most teens need eight to 10 hours of sleep.

1 Write two correct sentences for each picture.

I hate storms with heavy rain.
I hope this heat wave ends soon.
✓ I love blizzards.
I'm exhausted from working in the hot weather.
I'm stressed out from driving in bad weather.
I'm terrified of thunder and lightning.
It's wonderful to see all of the snow.
The hail is awful.

1. _I love blizzards._
   _____

2. _____
   _____

3. _____
   _____

4. _____
   _____

2 Complete the sentences with the simple present or simple past forms of the phrases.

do something creative
✓ not get enough sleep
not help around the house
shop for clothes
stay out late on the weekend
work out

1. I usually _don't get enough sleep_ during the week. I go to bed late and get up early.

2. I often _____. I hang out with friends Friday and Saturday nights.

3. Last week, my sister and I _____ at the mall. I spent $100.

4. Dan _____ at the gym for two hours yesterday.

5. They usually _____ when they're stressed out, like take photos.

6. Kelly _____ last weekend because she wasn't home.

3 Complete the sentences with the present continuous forms of the verbs. Then label each situation with the correct category.

Clothes and money	Entertainment	✓ Health care
	Food and drink	Transportation
Education		

1. The doctors _are helping_ (help) sick people in another country right now. _Health care_

2. Felipe _____ (study) law these days. _____

3. Shelly _____ (take) the bus right now because the train _____ (not run). _____

4. We _____ (have) sushi and tea in a Japanese restaurant right now.
   _____

5. Adam and Elsa _____ (watch) a comedy at the movie theater.
   _____

6. I _____ (not pay) for jeans and these T-shirts with cash. I _____ (use) my credit card.
   _____

4 Complete the paragraph with the simple past or past continuous forms of the verbs.

Last night, I ¹ __was sleeping__ (sleep) when it ² _____ (start) to rain. I ³ _____ (walk) to the window when I ⁴ _____ (hear) thunder. My parents ⁵ _____ (watch) a movie on TV when I ⁶ _____ (scream). They ⁷ _____ (run) to my room. They ⁸ _____ (wonder) what happened when they ⁹ _____ (see) that I was terrified of the thunder! After that, we ¹⁰ _____ (watch) the movie together, and then I ¹¹ _____ (go) to bed. I ¹² _____ (fall) asleep when my cat ¹³ _____ (jump) on my bed. I definitely ¹⁴ _____ (not get) enough sleep last night!

5 Circle the correct answers.

1. Julie is sick. She **had better** / had better not see a doctor.

2. We **must** / **must not** pay with a credit card. This restaurant only takes cash.

3. You **have to** / **don't have to** help around the house today. It's a mess!

4. Nelson and Ben **should** / **shouldn't** stay out so late. They're always exhausted in the morning.

5. We **ought to** / **ought not to** wear helmets when we ride our bikes on that road. It's dangerous.

6. You **must** / **must not** do your homework before you can hang out with friends.

7. Wendy **has to** / **doesn't have to** walk to school. She takes the bus.

8. You **had better** / **had better not** be late to class. The teacher is strict about being on time.

9. We **should** / **shouldn't** buy Tim a gift. It's his birthday tomorrow.

10. Ray **ought to** / **ought not to** drive without a license.

6 Write sentences with your own opinions. Use *It's (not)* + adjective + infinitive.

1. easy / ride / a bike

   It's easy to ride a bike. OR

   It's not easy to ride a bike.

2. fun / go / to amusement parks

   _____

3. smart / spend / money on an education

   _____

4. difficult / learn / English

   _____

5. important / have / time for yourself

   _____

6. hard / get / enough sleep

   _____

7. boring / watch TV / every weekend

   _____

7 Circle the correct answers.

1. **A:** Do you know how to fix a computer?
   B: No. _____

   a. I'm not very good at things like that.
   b. It's really pretty simple.

2. **A:** It's difficult to lift this heavy box.
   B: Wait. _____

   a. Let me show you.
   b. I'll give you a hand if you like.

3. **A:** It's hot in here. _____
   B: Yeah, but I like hot weather.

   a. I don't think so.
   b. Don't you think?

4. **A:** Our homework is confusing.
   B: I know. _____

   a. I'm not sure how to do it.
   b. I disagree.

5. **A:** I really want to beat this video game! Can you help me?
   B: Sure. _____

   a. I'm not very good at things like that.
   b. I'll give you a hand if you like.

6. **A:** Well, I'm glad we left at 6:00 like you wanted. These are great seats!
   B: _____ It's always good to go early.

   a. Don't you think?
   b. See what I mean?

3 Art All Around Us

1 Match the clues on the left with the things and people on the right. Some items have more than one answer.

1. a person __e__ , _____
2. done on a wall _____ , _____
3. done with a pencil _____
4. always done on a computer
   _____
5. a lot of art in one place
   _____
6. art made with the hands
   that isn't flat _____ , _____
7. usually in a book _____

a. digital art
b. pottery
c. exhibition
d. comics
e. living statue
f. mural
g. sculpture
h. drawing
i. portrait painter
j. graffiti

2 What kind of art are the materials below used for? Label the pictures with some of the words from Exercise 1.

1. _____pottery_____

2. _____

3. _____

4. _____

5. _____

6. _____

3 Complete the sentences with some of the words from Exercise 1.

1. A famous Diego Rivera _____ is at the Detroit Institute of Arts. It's a painting of factory workers painted on a wall in the museum.

2. My grandmother is a _____. She paints pictures of famous people.

3. I am a _____ in New York City. I dress up as the Statue of Liberty.

4. There's a great _____ of modern art at the museum.

4 Answer the questions with your own information.

1. What kind of art do you like to see at exhibitions?

   I like to see Renaissance art at exhibitions.

2. What kind of art do you have in your home or room?

   _____

3. Do you have an art class or did you take an art class in the past? What kind of art do/did you make?

   _____

4. Do you like comics? Why? / Why not?

   _____

1 Correct the sentences. Use the simple present and the -ing form of a verb (gerund).

1. John loves ~~go~~ _going_ to museums.

2. Isabel enjoying taking art classes.

3. We not like watching living statues. It's boring.

4. I don't mind to help my dad when he paints.

5. Cal and Vera hate draw pictures.

6. Marcia loves read comics. She reads them all the time.

2 Complete the two sentences about each picture with the correct verbs. Use the simple present and the *-ing* form of a verb.

| ✓ like | look | ✓ make | not enjoy |

1. Kate ___likes making___ pottery.

   She _____ at sculptures.

| hate | love | play | ride |

2. Joe _____ his skateboard.

   He _____ soccer.

| run | enjoy | not like | get |

3. Sparky _____ in the park.

   She _____ a bath.

| love | not mind | play | walk |

4. Dina and Ki _____ soccer in the

   park. They _____ to school.

3 Put the words in order to make sentences. Change the correct verbs to the *-ing* form.

1. enjoy / on the weekends / Stacey / shop / for clothes

   Stacey enjoys shopping for clothes

   on the weekends.

2. camp / and Dan / in the mountains / Tyler / love

   _____

   _____

3. to / go / I / art exhibitions / don't enjoy

   _____

   _____

4. around / don't mind / the house / we / help

   _____

   _____

5. of her cat / Donna / paint / loves / portraits

   _____

   _____

6. watch / hate / horror movies / you

   _____

   _____

4 Write sentences that are true for you with the simple present and the *-ing* form of a verb. Use the phrases *(not) like, (not) love, hate, (not) enjoy,* or *not mind.*

1. ride a bike

   I love riding a bike.

2. go to museums

   _____

3. watch living statues

   _____

4. draw pictures

   _____

5. take photos

   _____

6. help around the house

   _____

VOCABULARY Musical instruments

1 Look at the pictures and complete the crossword.

ACROSS

2.

5.

6.

7.

8.

9.

10.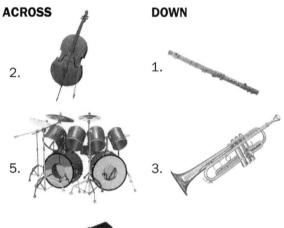

DOWN

1.

3.

4.

2 Check (✓) the items that are true for each instrument. Sometimes more than one answer is possible.

	You use your mouth to play this.	You use your hands to play this.	It has strings.
1. a trumpet	✓	✓	
2. drums			
3. a guitar			
4. a keyboard			
5. a cello			
6. a piano			
7. a flute			
8. a harmonica			
9. a violin			
10. a saxophone			

3 Look at the pictures in Exercise 1 again. Write sentences about the instruments the people are playing. Use the present continuous.

1. *Tia is playing a guitar.*

2. _____

3. _____

4. _____

5. _____

6. _____

GRAMMAR *-ing* forms (gerunds) as subjects

1 Write the *-ing* forms of the verbs.

1. draw _____*drawing*_____

2. take _____

3. run _____

4. make _____

5. feel _____

6. shop _____

7. care _____

8. play _____

2 Complete the sentences with the *-ing* forms of the verbs from Exercise 1.

1. _____*Drawing*_____ outside is very relaxing.

2. _____ the drums loudly is fun.

3. _____ for animals is a big responsibility.

4. _____ is really good exercise.

5. _____ for clothes can take a lot of time.

6. _____ pottery is harder than it looks.

7. _____ photos is Sonya's favorite thing to do.

8. _____ exhausted is not good for you.

3 Write the activities in the order you like doing them. Use the *-ing* forms of the verbs. 1 = the activity you like the best.

chat with friends
do something creative
play a musical instrument
ride on a roller coaster
visit a museum

1. _____

2. _____

3. _____

4. _____

5. _____

Verbs + prepositions + *-ing* forms (gerunds)

4 Write sentences. Use verbs + prepositions + *-ing* forms.

1. not apologize / for / make / mistakes isn't a good idea

   Not apologizing for making mistakes

   isn't a good idea.

2. you need to / concentrate / on / study

   _____

3. our lessons / consist / of / make / pottery and jewelry

   _____

4. Janice / feel / like / play / her guitar right now

   _____

5. not believe / in / have / time for yourself can have negative results

   _____

6. I / decide / against / go / to the concert

   _____

5 Answer the questions with your own ideas. Use *-ing* forms as subjects or use a verb + a preposition + the *-ing* form of a verb.

1. What do you think about painting?

   Painting is hard, but some people are

   good at it.

2. When do you concentrate on studying?

   _____

3. What's your opinion about exercising?

   _____

4. What do you worry about?

   _____

5. What have you apologized for doing?

   _____

6. What do you think about learning to play an instrument?

   _____

1 Circle the correct words.

1. **How** / **Should** about going to the Museum of Modern Art tomorrow?

2. **How** / **What** time should we meet?

3. **Should** / **Sounds** good.

4. **What** / **Should** I ask my brother to take us?

5. **That's** / **Sounding** a good idea.

2 Complete the conversation with the phrases from Exercise 1.

Mateo: Hi, Sara. 1 *How about going to the Museum of Modern Art tomorrow?*

Sara: Really? I thought you hated going to museums.

Mateo: Well, I usually do, but there's a really cool digital art exhibition. They have pictures of skateboarders that an artist created on a computer.

Sara: Cool! I'd like seeing that.

Mateo: OK. The museum is kind of far, but we can ride our bikes.

Sara: 2 _____ He won't mind driving.

Mateo: 3 _____ I can come to your house then. 4 _____

Sara: Well, he doesn't like getting up early. How about 11:00 a.m.?

Mateo: 5 _____

READING TO WRITE

1 Answer the questions with information from the poster.

ROCK WITH US!

DOKK **is playing this Friday!**

Come and hear our new songs on Friday, April 10, at 9:00 p.m. at Newtown Park.

1. What's the name of the band?

   _____

2. What kind of music do they play?

   _____

3. When are they playing?

   _____

4. Where are they playing?

   _____

2 Circle the correct words.

Gina: How ¹(**was**) / **were** the concert last night?

Barry: It ²**was** / **were** great! I love listening to live music.

Gina: Who played?

Barry: DOKK. The band's name ³**is** / **are** from the first letters of the members' names – Donna, Olivia, Kevin, and Kim.

Gina: Cool. Where ⁴**is** / **are** the band from?

Barry: They ⁵**is** / **are** from Austin, Texas. They write their own music. Donna ⁶**is** / **are** an amazing drummer, Kevin and Kim play the guitar, and Olivia sings. Last night, they ⁷**was** / **were** amazing! I liked the concert because they played my favorite songs, and they played their new songs, too.

Gina: ⁸**Is** / **Are** it your favorite band?

Barry: Well, no. My favorite band ⁹**is** / **are** The Three Joshes, but I like DOKK a lot. They ¹⁰**is** / **are** really popular. There ¹¹**was** / **were** a big crowd last night. I think there ¹²**was** / **were** over 500 people at the concert.

Gina: Wow! Next time they play, let me know, and I'll go with you.

3 Complete Barry's blog post about the concert. Use the information in the poster from Exercise 1 and the conversation from Exercise 2.

○○○

LAST WEEKEND'S CONCERT

Posted on April 8

I went to a great concert last weekend at

¹ _Newtown Park_ . There were ² _____ people

at the concert. Most of them were teenagers. A band named

³ _____ played. They are a ⁴ _____

band from Austin, ⁵ _____ . There are

⁶ _____ people in the band. Their band name

is from ⁷ _____ of their names. The concert was

⁸ _____ ! I liked it because they played my

⁹ _____ . Their ¹⁰ _____ were also

really good. If they play in your city, you have to go see

this band!

4 *Sign Me Up!*

VOCABULARY Adventure travel

1 Find eight more words associated with travel activities.

N	H	I	M	H	K	C	C	A	M	W	U	M	K	M
B	B	S	O	Z	J	R	A	F	T	I	N	G	Q	N
T	B	L	U	N	B	U	I	C	R	U	I	S	E	Z
O	A	I	N	M	D	I	Y	B	N	A	B	N	L	R
S	C	U	T	I	G	Z	I	N	G	Y	A	T	A	O
H	K	S	A	I	L	I	N	G	P	G	L	E	S	C
M	P	F	I	Y	C	B	Q	X	A	G	L	R	L	K
R	A	S	N	R	H	I	Q	U	R	B	O	M	M	C
G	C	Z	B	C	K	M	O	U	N	F	O	Y	O	L
T	K	Y	I	X	D	E	P	C	N	E	N	A	T	I
D	I	W	K	N	X	S	A	F	A	R	I	F	P	M
G	N	K	I	S	I	S	L	E	R	P	N	E	S	B
I	G	X	N	T	S	A	F	A	N	A	G	S	U	I
Y	P	Y	G	B	Q	F	N	H	B	O	G	P	F	N
T	S	U	M	M	E	R	C	A	M	P	D	I	A	G

2 Check (✓) the activities that involve water.

1. ❏ go backpacking
2. ❏ go on a cruise
3. ❏ go ballooning
4. ❏ go mountain biking
5. ❏ go on a safari
6. ❏ go rafting
7. ❏ go rock climbing
8. ❏ go sailing
9. ❏ go to summer camp

3 Complete Javier's email with some of the expressions from Exercise 2. Use the simple past.

To Tim
From Javier
Subject My summer at camp

Hey Tim,

I'm so glad that I ¹ ___*went to summer camp*___ .
At first, I didn't want to be away from home this summer, but I'm having a great time. There are a lot of cool activities here. Last week, we ² _____ on the lake. We took two boats so that everyone at camp could go. We also ³ _____ on the Red River. It was very fast! I ⁴ _____, too. I had to wear a helmet and use ropes to get to the top of the mountain!
On Saturday, we ⁵ _____.
My bag was really heavy because I brought a lot of water and food for the hike. On Sunday, we ⁶ _____ on some trails. I was glad that I brought my bike to camp, so I didn't have to rent one.

Yesterday was the best! We ⁷ _____. It was amazing! We were so high up in the sky.

I can't believe that you ⁸ _____. Did you see any elephants, lions, or giraffes? Write soon and tell me all about your trip.

Your friend,

Javier

4 Answer the questions with your own information.

1. Which activities from Exercise 2 have you done?
   I have gone rafting, and I have gone on a cruise.
   _____

2. Which activities would you like to do?
   _____

3. Which activities wouldn't you want to try?
   _____

Present perfect with
already, yet, and just; **present perfect questions**

1 Read the sentences. Circle the answer that correctly explains each situation.

1. The boat hasn't left yet.

   a. The boat left.   (b. The boat didn't leave.)

2. They've already left for summer camp.

   a. They are at home.   b. They aren't at home.

3. We have just seen lions on a safari.

   a. We saw lions a few   b. We saw lions a
      minutes ago.   week ago.

4. They haven't cleaned the boat yet.

   a. They won't clean   b. They will probably
      the boat.   clean the boat later.

5. Calvin has just told me about his trip.

   a. Calvin told me about   b. Calvin told me about
      his trip recently.   his trip a while ago.

2 Rewrite the sentences and questions with the words in parentheses.

1. Have you left the house? (yet)

   Have you left the house yet?

2. I have told Todd our travel plans. (already)

   _____

3. Jenna has taken a picture of a monkey. (just)

   _____

4. They haven't gone rafting. (yet)

   _____

5. Has Sheila called you? (yet)

   _____

3 Put the words in order to make sentences.

1. decided / rafting / just / to go / we / have

   We have just decided to go rafting.

2. about / already / sailing / seen / that
   documentary / I / have

   _____

   _____

3. his / Peng / packed / yet / hasn't / bags /

   _____

   _____

4. have / already / the cruise / for / my parents /
   left

   _____

   _____

5. summer camp / has / from / Carolina / gotten
   back / just

   _____

   _____

6. about / you / your / yet / told me / trip / haven't

   _____

   _____

4 Look at the picture. Write sentences about Emma's activities. Use *already* and *yet*.

To Do
buy sunglasses
call my grandma ✓

1. pack her suitcase

   Emma has packed her suitcase already.

2. pack her tablet

   She _____

3. shut down her tablet

   _____

4. clean her room

   _____

5. buy sunglasses

   _____

6. call her grandma

   _____

VOCABULARY Phrasal verbs related to travel

1. Complete the sentences with a word or phrase from each box.

come	✓look
find	look
give	make
look	take

around	✓out
back	out
forward to	sure
off	up

1. ___*Look out*___! That rock is going to fall.

2. We're closed. Please _____ tomorrow.

3. I want to _____ more about rock climbing in this area.

4. Don't _____. With a little practice, you'll be great at mountain biking.

5. Our plane will _____ in about an hour.

6. Please _____ you wear a helmet when you're biking.

7. Many people _____ summer vacation.

8. Let's _____ the nature center after we hike.

2 Correct the sentences.

1. I'm not looking forward ~~of~~ *to* going home.

2. Sharon has already found in about the rock climbing class.

3. You need to take sure you wear hiking boots on the trails.

4. I don't want to give out, but this is really hard.

5. Did your plane take up on time?

6. David hasn't looked back from Ecuador yet.

7. I want to go to the market and find around a little.

3 Complete the quiz questions with some of the phrasal verbs from Exercise 1. Then circle the answers that are true for you.

1. Who ___*makes sure*___ you get up on time?

   a. I do.
   b. My parents.
   c. My brother or sister.

2. What do you _____ the most?

   a. Vacation.
   b. Weekends.
   c. Concerts.

3. When do you _____ on something?

   a. Never!
   b. When it is too hard.
   c. When it takes too much time.

4. Which of these things would you most like to _____ about?

   a. Nature trails in my area.
   b. Rock climbing adventures.
   c. Sailing classes.

5. When do you like to _____ in a store the most?

   a. When I'm buying something for myself.
   b. When I'm buying something for my family.
   c. When I'm buying something for a friend.

GRAMMAR Present perfect with *for* and *since*

1 Write the expressions in the correct places in the chart. Add *for* or *since*.

✓a week	last Tuesday	2013	a month
two days	5:00 p.m.	six hours	April

for	since
for a week	

2 Circle the correct words.

1. Lia has been a rock climbing instructor **for** / (**since**) 2010.

2. Jordan's been in Jamaica **for** / **since** two weeks.

3. You haven't called me **for** / **since** three days.

4. Britt hasn't been rafting **for** / **since** July.

5. I haven't seen Marcos **for** / **since** 3:00.

6. Have you been studying **for** / **since** an hour?

3 Complete the paragraph with the present perfect forms of the verbs and *for* or *since*.

○○○

River Valley Summer Camp

Join us this summer at our wonderful camp. River Valley Summer Camp [1] *has been open* (be open) *since* 2001. Hundreds of teens [2] _____ (enjoy) our camp _____ over 10 years.

Meet Martin: He [3] _____ (be) a camp leader _____ 2012. He [4] _____ (teach) rafting classes _____ five years. This year, he will lead our new river rafting adventures.

Meet Aya: She [5] _____ (cook) delicious meals for our camp _____ last June. You'll love the food at River Valley.

Meet Max and Judy: They [6] _____ (know) each other _____ eight years. They met at River Valley eight years ago, and they got married last year. Now they run the sailing classes together.

[7] _____ you _____ (want) to come to a summer camp _____ a long time? Sign up for River Valley today!

How long . . . ? and the present perfect

4 Look at Eric's activities. Write questions with *How long* and the present perfect. Then answer the questions.

live in Kenya	2009
work at a nature center	two years
be a safari guide	a month
teach nature classes	July
have his website about safaris	2012

1. *How long has Eric lived in Kenya?*
   He's lived in Kenya since 2009.

2. _____

   _____

3. _____

   _____

4. _____

   _____

5. _____

   _____

5 Answer the questions with your own information.

1. How long have you lived in your city?
   I've lived in my city since I was five years old.

2. How long has your family lived in your house?
   _____

3. How long have you been a student?
   _____

4. How long have you studied English?
   _____

5. How long have you and your best friend known each other?
   _____

6. How long have you owned a computer?
   _____

CONVERSATION Signing up for an adventure activity

1 Circle the correct phrases.

Emily: Hello. ¹**Does the price include /
Can I ask you a few things about** the
ballooning trip?

Guide: Sure. What would you like to know?

Emily: ²**How long is / Where can I sign up**
the trip?

Guide: It's from 2:00 to 6:00, but you're only
in the air for about two hours. First,
we give you safety information about
ballooning.

Emily: OK. ³**What about / Is it only for**
adults?

Guide: No. But if you're under 18, an adult
must be with you.

Emily: I see. ⁴**What do I need to bring /
Where can I sign up?**

Guide: Not much. But you should wear a
jacket. It can be cold up in the air. It's
an amazing experience.

Emily: ⁵**How long is / What about** cameras?
Can I bring mine?

Guide: Of course. You just have to be really
careful with it. You don't want it to fall
out of the balloon!

**2 Complete the conversation with the correct
phrases.**

> ✓Can I ask you a few things about
> Does the price include
> How long is
> Is it only for
> Where can I sign up

Noah: ¹ *Can I ask you a few things about*
the rock climbing trip?

Guide: Of course.

Noah: ² _____
experienced climbers?

Guide: No, not at all. It's for beginners, too.

Noah: Great. ³_____
equipment?

Guide: Yes, it does. We provide helmets, knee
pads, and everything else you need.

Noah: OK. ⁴_____ it?

Guide: You can choose a two-hour or four-hour
adventure. It's a lot of fun, and our
guides will help you with everything.

Noah: Sounds great.
⁵_____ ?

Guide: Right here!

READING TO WRITE

1 Read the sentences that compare house parties in Ecuador and the United States. Match the sentences that are about the same topics.

Ecuador	The United States
1. People wait for the host to serve them food. _d_	a. Guests sometimes bring food to the party.
2. People usually play music and dance. ___	b. Parties can be big or small.
3. The host usually makes all of the food. ___	c. Most people dress casually.
4. Younger people often wear informal clothing, but older people often dress up. ___	d. The host often puts food on a table, and guests help themselves.
5. Parties are various sizes – from a few people to many friends. ___	e. People often listen to music while they talk.

2 Complete the sentences with the correct words.

also	either . . . or
although	however
✓ both . . . and	not only . . . but also . . .

¹ __Both__ people from South America ___and___ Asia often shake hands when they greet people from the United States or Canada.

When people in Asia meet for the first time, they often give each other business cards. ² _____ people in South America don't always give each other business cards, they may exchange phone numbers and emails.

In South America, people ³ _____ kiss each other on the cheek _____ hug each other. In Asia, ⁴ _____, people do not touch each other when they say hello. They bow. ⁵ _____ do they bow when they say hello, _____ they _____ bow when they say goodbye.

3 Write the pieces of the article from Exercise 2 under the correct headings.

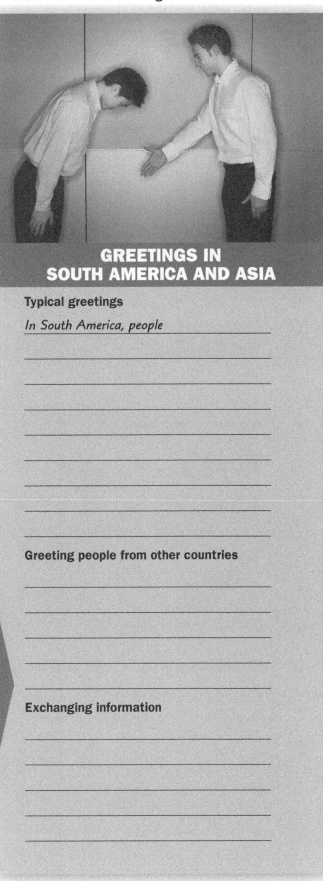

GREETINGS IN SOUTH AMERICA AND ASIA

Typical greetings

In South America, people _____

_____

_____

_____

_____

_____

_____

_____

_____

Greeting people from other countries

_____

_____

_____

_____

Exchanging information

_____

_____

_____

_____

_____

1 Look at the pictures and complete the puzzle. Find out what John did on vacation by filling in the gray boxes.

John went _____ on vacation.

	1				
	c	r	u	i	s	e

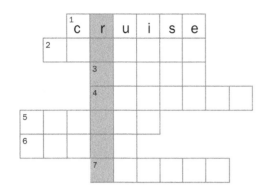

1.
2.
3.
4.
5.
6.
7.

2 Write the words in the correct places in the chart.

backpacking	graffiti	a safari
ballooning	a harmonica	sailing
a cello	✓ a mural	a saxophone
drums	pottery	a sculpture

Art	Music	Travel
a mural	_____	_____
_____	_____	_____
_____	_____	_____
_____	_____	_____

3 Complete the sentences with the simple present forms of the phrases. Use a verb + -*ing* form (gerund).

> hate / come back
> ✓ love / find out
> not enjoy / make sure
> not like / give up
> not mind / look around

1. Lauren ____*loves finding out*____ about new places.

2. Terrance _____ home after vacation.

3. I _____ when I try something new.

4. My brother _____ when I go shopping.

5. My mother _____ I've done my chores.

4 Complete the sentences with the -*ing* forms of the verbs. Add a preposition when necessary.

[1] ____*Being*____ (be) a portrait painter is an amazing job. I love it, and I think [2] ____*about drawing*____ (draw) all the time! I studied digital art in high school, but in college, I concentrated [3] _____ (learn) to draw. [4] _____ (not follow) my dream would have been a mistake. Now my work consists [5] _____ (paint) portraits of interesting people. [6] _____ (work) with new people can be difficult. They have to sit for hours, and [7] _____ (sit) still is difficult, especially for children. My clients may get tired, but I don't worry [8] _____ (be) bored. I love my job, and I always will!

5 Look at Alexis's To Do list. Then complete sentences about her activities. Use the present perfect with *already* and *yet*. ✓ = She's done it.

TO DO:

✓ *go to the photo exhibition with Anna*

practice the violin

pack clothes for summer camp

✓ *buy my dad's birthday present*

help around the house with Josh

✓ *do my homework*

1. Alexis and Anna _have already gone to the photo exhibition._

2. Alexis _____

3. She _____

4. She _____

5. Alexis and Josh _____

_____

6. Alexis _____

6 Complete the conversation with the present perfect forms of the verbs and *already*, *yet*, or *just*.

Rick: Hey, Carla. ¹___*Have*___ you ___*had*___ dinner ___*yet*___? (have / yet)

Carla: No, I ²_____. But I ³_____ _____ _____ lunch. (finish / just)

Rick: Oh, OK. Well, do you want to go out for dinner in a few hours?

Carla: Sounds good. ⁴_____ you _____ at that new Mexican restaurant _____? (eat / yet)

Rick: Yes, I ⁵_____. I ⁶_____ _____ _____ there three times. (be / already)

Carla: But ⁷_____ you _____ the chicken tostadas _____? (try / yet)

Rick: No, I ⁸_____. Let's go and I'll try them!

7 Write questions for the answers. Then complete the answers with *for* or *since*.

1. _How long has she been on a safari?_

She's been on a safari ___*for*___ ten days.

2. _____

They've lived in Chicago _____ 2006.

3. _____

I've played the saxophone _____ six months.

4. _____

We've known Raul _____ three years.

5. _____

He's worked at the summer camp _____ June.

8 Complete the conversations with the correct phrases.

Does the price include

✓ How about going

How long is

Is it only for

What do I need to bring

What time should we meet

1. A: What do you want to do today?

B: ___*How about going*___ to the digital art exhibition at the museum?

2. A: _____ the backpacking trip?

B: Five days.

3. A: _____?

B: A warm jacket and hiking boots.

4. A: _____ transportation?

B: Yes, it does. We take you to the river on a bus.

5. A: _____ beginners?

B: No, it isn't. We have classes for advanced climbers.

6. A: _____?

B: How about 6:00 p.m.?

5 Yikes!

VOCABULARY Fears

1 **Circle seven more words about fears.**

cthedarksnaelevatorstsngpqflyingbirectclownsvathoptdsnakesingheiinsectstgifpsmnheightsabtwlfqpbirdsflatnf

2 **Look at the pictures. Complete the sentences with the correct fears from Exercise 1.**

1. Tao and Sherry are afraid of ____heights____, and they're afraid of _____.

2. Vic is afraid of _____ and _____.

3. Alicia is afraid of _____ and _____.

4. Ed is afraid of _____ and _____.

3 **Circle the correct words in the quiz. Then check (✓) the answers that are true for you. Add your points.**

How fearful are you?

	Always true 3 points	Sometimes true 2 points	Never true 1 point
1 I take the stairs because I hate riding in ⊙elevators / **the dark**.			
2 I don't like hiking because **snakes / flying** scare me.			
3 I don't go to the circus because I'm afraid of **insects / clowns**.			
4 I can't walk on high bridges because I'm afraid of **heights / clowns**.			
5 I sleep with a nightlight because I'm afraid of **heights / the dark**.			
6 **Snakes / Birds** scare me when they fly over my head.			
7 I'm afraid of **elevators / flying**. I hate planes!			
8 I don't like to sit on the ground because I'm afraid of **insects / birds**.			

My points: _____

17–24 points: You're afraid of a lot of things. It can stop you from doing things.

9–16 points: You have some fears, but you can probably overcome them.

8 points: You aren't afraid of anything!

1 Read the sentences and check (✓) the correct columns.

	Planned event	Decided at the moment of speaking
1. Hey, I think I'll go to the store with you.		✓
2. Paul is going to study in Mexico next year.		
3. I'm not working on Saturday.		
4. I don't know the answer. Janice will tell you.		
5. Sean is taking a test in an hour.		
6. I'm not going to go on the camping trip because I'm afraid of insects.		
7. No, I won't hike to the top of the mountain. I'm afraid of heights.		
8. Sakura is going to take a class about facing fears.		

2 Rewrite the sentences. Change the present continuous to *be going to* and use the words in parentheses.

1. Sandra is shopping with Rachel tomorrow. (next week)

   Sandra is going to shop with Rachel

   next week.

2. My brother is getting married in two days. (next year)

   _____

3. We are going to Rio de Janeiro next week. (in April)

   _____

4. I'm talking to the teacher in a few minutes. (after class)

   _____

5. Pam is going on a safari on Monday. (next month)

   _____

6. They're watching a movie tonight. (on Saturday)

   _____

3 Complete the conversations with the correct forms of *will* and the words in parentheses.

1. **A:** What are you going to do tomorrow?

   B: I don't know. Maybe _____ *I'll go* _____ (I / go) to the mall.

2. **A:** Do you and Don want to go to dinner with me after class?

   B: Sure. _____ (we / eat) with you.

3. **A:** Can I borrow your tablet?

   B: Sorry, I need it. But _____ (I / give) it to you when I'm done.

4. **A:** Where are you going on vacation?

   B: I'm not sure, but _____ (we / not choose) somewhere cold.

5. **A:** Do you want to take the elevator?

   B: No! I hate elevators. _____ (I / take) the stairs.

First conditional

4 Complete the paragraph with the first conditional.

Rita is afraid of snakes. If she
1_____ *sees* _____ (see) a snake, she
2_____ (not move).
If the snake 3_____ (move), she
4_____ (scream). If she
5_____ (scream), her brother
6_____ (hear) her. If Rita's
brother 7_____ (see) her with
the snake, he 8_____ (not help).
If he 9_____ (laugh), Rita
10_____ (cry). I hope Rita
doesn't see a snake!

1 Complete the chart.

	-ed	-ing
1.	embarrassed	*embarrassing*
2.		confusing
3.	interested	
4.		surprising
5.	exhausted	
6.		terrifying
7.	disgusted	
8.		relaxing

2 Complete the sentences with some of the words from Exercise 1. Then check (✓) if the sentences are true for you.

	Yes	No
1. I think space is _interesting_. There's always something new to learn about.		
2. I always feel _____ at the beach. The sound of the ocean makes me feel calm.		
3. Exercising is _____. I'm always tired after I work out.		
4. Yuck! I think snakes are _____.		
5. I was _____ on my last birthday! My parents had a party for me and invited all of my friends.		
6. I was _____ about my last test scores. I didn't do very well.		
7. I think clowns are _____. They really scare me.		
8. I'm never _____ in class. I always understand everything!		

3 Complete the sentences with the -ed or -ing adjective of the words in parentheses.

1. Martina is ___*disgusted*___ (disgust) by insects.

2. Henry was _____ (exhaust) after he walked up eight flights of stairs.

3. Lori thinks her parents are _____ (embarrass) when they yell at her soccer games.

4. My little sister is _____ (terrify) of sleeping in the dark.

5. It was _____ (surprise) to find out Tara moved to Los Angeles.

6. Our homework assignment was _____ (confuse). No one understood the directions.

7. I'm not very _____ (interest) in science, but I love math.

8. Some people are afraid of flying, but I think it's _____ (relax).

GRAMMAR Modals of probability: *must, can't, may, might, could*

1 Read the sentences and check (✓) the correct columns.

	Almost certain	Impossible	Possible
1. Ramon must be from Mexico.	✓		
2. I might not have homework this weekend.			
3. We may not work tomorrow.			
4. Hillary can't be 16.			
5. My cousin could be at the mall.			
6. You must be exhausted.			

2 Match the sentences.

1. Laura wasn't in class today. _c_	a. She may not be hungry.
2. Kelly won't ride on roller coasters. _____	b. She could be busy.
3. Laila doesn't speak Japanese. _____	c. She might be sick.
4. Beth didn't order anything to eat. _____	d. She must be terrified of heights.
5. Nancy just ran 5 kilometers. _____	e. She can't be from Japan.
6. Mari didn't answer her phone. _____	f. She must be exhausted.

3 Complete the conversation with *must*, *can't*, or *might*.

Julia: Do you know where Kayla is?

Mike: No, I don't. She ____might____ be sick.

Julia: No, she ²_____ be sick. I talked to her this morning. She said she was coming to the party.

Mike: Hmm. How is she getting here?

Julia: She's taking the bus and then walking.

Mike: The bus ³_____ be late. It's usually on time, but you never know!

Julia: That ⁴_____ be true. She was already on the bus when I talked to her.

Mike: I see. Well, she ⁵_____ have to stop at the store on her way.

Julia: Oh, yeah! That ⁶_____ be it! She said she hadn't gotten a birthday card for Jacob yet.

Mike: Ah. Hey, do you think Jacob will be surprised?

Julia: I'm not sure. He ⁷_____ know about the party.

Mike: Really?

Julia: Yeah. His brother ⁸_____ keep a secret!

4 Write sentences with *must*, *can't*, or *may*.

1. Jenna / be / cold

   Jenna must be cold.

2. Isaac / go / rafting / or / go / ballooning

   _____

3. Jin-hee / be / finished with her book

   _____

4. You / be / exhausted

   _____

5. Nicole / fall off / her bike

   _____

5 Rewrite the sentences. Add the words in parentheses.

1. Paul is surprised. (might)

   Paul might be surprised.

2. It's 3:00. (must)

   _____

3. Cindy knows Julia. (could)

   _____

4. That roller coaster is terrifying. (must)

   _____

5. We expect to win the race. (can't)

   _____

6. You have the flu. (could)

   _____

1 Complete the phrases in the conversation.

Raul: Hi, Sofia. My friends and I are hiking up Cotopaxi this weekend.

Sofia: ¹N _o_ w _a_ _y_! That's cool.

Raul: Do you want to come?

Sofia: Sure. I'd love to! Can I invite Carolina?

Raul: Well, I don't know if she'd want to come. Cotopaxi is snowy once you get up high.

Sofia: So?

Raul: Well, Carolina is afraid of snow.

Sofia: ²T__ __ __'s im__ __ __ __ __ __ __ __!
No one is afraid of snow.

Raul: It's true. There's even a name for it – chinophobia.

Sofia: Chinophobia? ³A__ __ y__ __
s __ __ __ __ __ __?

Raul: Yes, I am. It's a real thing, and Carolina has it.

Sofia: ⁴I d__ __'t b__ __ __ __ __ __ i__!

Raul: It's true. We were looking at this picture of snow one time, and she got really nervous.

Sofia: ⁵C__ __ __ o__! She got nervous just looking at snow?

Raul: Yes, she did!

Sofia: I'm going to call and ask her about it!

2 Circle the correct answers.

1. **A:** I climbed Cotopaxi in an hour.
   B: No **possible** / **way**! It takes expert climbers several hours.

2. **A:** Marcia is living in Quito for a year.
   B: Are you **serious** / **believing**? That's great.

3. **A:** Jorge took 10 bottles of water on the hike.
   B: **Believe** / **Come** on. His bag would have been too heavy.

4. **A:** Yolanda moved from the mountains to downtown Quito.
   B: I don't **impossible** / **believe** you. She hates busy cities.

5. **A:** There wasn't any snow on the top of Cotopaxi when we climbed it.
   B: That's **possible** / **impossible**. There's always snow on Cotopaxi.

1 Circle the correct expressions.

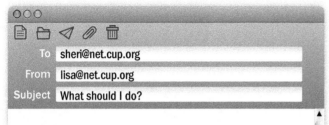

To sheri@net.cup.org
From lisa@net.cup.org
Subject What should I do?

Hello Sheri,

Thanks for writing. Your summer plans sound fun. ¹**Check this out / The fact**: I'm going to go to summer camp this year. It's in the mountains, and it's going to be really fun. The ²**problem / idea** is that we live for a month without any modern technology – no cell phones, no tablets, no lights! Cool, right? ³**The problem is that / Listen to** I promised to text my little sister every day. I haven't told her that I can't yet. I'm a little nervous to tell her because I know she's going to be upset. The ⁴**idea / truth** is that I'm looking forward to not using my phone, but I just don't know what to say to my sister. What do you think I should do?

Your friend,

Lisa

2 Match the categories with the sentences from Lisa's email.

1. _d_ Greeting	a. I haven't told her that I can't yet.
2. _____ Personal news	b. What do you think I should do?
3. _____ The problem	c. I promised to text my little sister every day.
4. _____ How you feel about the problem and why	d. Hello Sheri,
5. _____ What you have/ haven't done about the problem	e. I'm going to summer camp.
6. _____ A question to ask what your friend thinks	f. I'm a little nervous to tell her because I know she's going to be upset.

3 Write the email in the correct order.

Because of this, I don't think I can go to the festival.

Kevin

I'm really embarrassed, and I haven't told him yet.

Your friend,

The problem is that I have acousticophobia – I'm afraid of loud noises.

What do you think I should say to him?

✓ Hi Victor,

Check this out: My cousin's band is going to play in a music festival next month.

To victor@net.cup.org
From kevin@net.cup.org
Subject A problem

Hi Victor,

_____

_____

_____

_____

_____

_____

_____

_____

_____

_____

_____

6 Difficult Decisions

School life

1 Complete the sentences and the crossword.

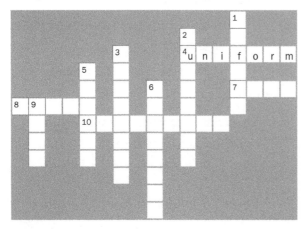

ACROSS

4. I don't mind wearing a ____uniform____ to school.

7. Many students aren't following the dress _____.

8. We're trying to win a _____ for "best project."

10. Sara was assigned to _____ for being late.

DOWN

1. Jack got sent to the principal's _____ for talking in class.

2. _____ is not allowed at our school. We must be kind to each other.

3. Tim was caught _____ on a test.

5. I'm getting extra _____ in my English class.

6. I'm always _____. I'm never late for class.

9. Our teacher talked to us about not being _____. She said we have to be more polite.

2 Complete the paragraph with the correct words or phrases.

be assigned	cheating
be punctual	follow
✓ be rude	get sent
bullying	wear

Hampton High School RULES

Do not [1] ____be rude____ to teachers or other students. [2] _____ is not allowed. Students must treat each other kindly. Students who are disrespectful will [3] _____ to the principal's office.

You must [4] _____. If you are late more than three times in one month, you'll [5] _____ to detention.

There is absolutely no [6] _____. Students must do their own work.

All students must [7] _____ the dress code. You have to [8] _____ school uniforms.

3 Answer the questions with your own information.

1. Does your school have a dress code? Do you have to wear school uniforms?

   Our school has a dress code. Everyone has
   to wear a white shirt and black pants.

2. Why do students at your school get sent to the principal's office? Why are they assigned to detention?

   _____

   _____

3. Do you ever get extra credit in your classes? Which classes?

   _____

   _____

GRAMMAR Second conditional

1 Correct the second conditional sentences.

1. If I ~~would change~~ *changed* our school's dress code, I'd let students wear jeans every day.

2. If you bullied a student, you be assigned to detention.

3. If Sara does the best in the contest, she'd win the prize.

4. If we wasn't punctual, our teacher would be upset.

5. My teacher sends me to the principal's office if I broke the school rules.

6. Luke wouldn't pass the test if he not study.

7. Debbie would tell the teacher if she would see someone cheating.

8. I'd go to the soccer game I didn't have to study.

2 Complete the paragraph with the second conditional.

If Tim [1] _____ *bullied* _____ (bully) students,
he [2] _____ (be) assigned to detention.
If he [3] _____ (be) assigned to detention,
his parents [4] _____ (be) angry. If his
parents [5] _____ (be) angry, they
[6] _____ (make) him do chores. If Tim
[7] _____ (have) to do chores, he
[8] _____ (not be) happy. Tim had better
not bully students!

3 Write second conditional sentences with the information in the chart.

	Imaginary situation	Possible consequence
1.	Leo / fail / his test	his parents / be / angry
2.	You / not call me	I / wonder / why
3.	Carla / win / the prize	she / be / happy
4.	Mark and Doug / not have / class	they / go / to the concert
5.	Jenny / go / on vacation	she / miss / her classes
6.	I / be rude / to my classmates	I / get sent / to the principal's office

1. *If Leo failed his test, his parents would be angry.*
2. _____
3. _____
4. _____
5. _____
6. _____

Second conditional *yes/no* questions

4 Write second conditional questions. Then answer the questions with your own information.

1. if / your friends / go / to a concert / your parents / let / you go with them

Q: *If your friends went to a concert, would your parents let you go with them?*

A: *Yes, they would.*   OR *No, they wouldn't.*

2. if / your friend / bully / another student / you / tell / the principal

Q: _____

A: _____

3. you / apologize / if / you / be / rude to a classmate

Q: _____

A: _____

4. your parents / be / angry / if / you / cheat / on a test

Q: _____

A: _____

VOCABULARY Expressions with *make* and *do*

1 Write the expressions in the correct places in the chart. Add *make* or *do*.

a difference	research
friends	something fun
✓ homework	the right thing
me a favor	you mad

do	make
do homework	_____
_____	_____
_____	_____
_____	
_____	

2 Complete the sentences with the correct expressions from Exercise 1.

1. Jacob likes to ___*do the right thing*___ at school. He always follows the rules.

2. Charlotte is very friendly, and it's easy for her to _____.

3. Kyle really wants to _____ at his school. He started a "stop bullying" group.

4. I want to _____ this weekend. Let's go sailing!

5. Can you _____? I need help with my homework.

6. I never want to _____. I don't like it when you're angry.

7. My sister likes to _____ for school projects. She loves learning new things.

8. I can't go to the park. I have to _____.

3 Circle the correct words. Then write answers with your own information.

1. How often do you (do) / make homework? Where do you (do) / make it?

   I do homework every night. I do it at my desk.

2. Have you ever **done / made** a favor for someone? What did you **do / make**?

   _____

   _____

   _____

3. Do you **do / make** research online? When?

   _____

   _____

   _____

4. When do you **do / make** something fun? What do you **do / make**?

   _____

   _____

   _____

5. Do you **do / make** friends easily? How do you **do / make** new friends?

   _____

   _____

   _____

6. When your friends break the rules, do you **do / make** the right thing? What do you **do / make**?

   _____

   _____

   _____

7. Who **does / makes** you mad? Why?

   _____

   _____

   _____

8. Have you ever **done / made** a difference at your school? What was it?

   _____

   _____

   _____

GRAMMAR Second conditional *Wh-* questions

1 Match the questions with the answers.

1. What would you do if you didn't finish your homework? ___*d*___	a. I'd go in August.
2. Who would you tell if someone bullied you at school? _____	b. I'd make new friends.
3. How would you do research if you had to write a paper? _____	c. I'd find information online.
4. If you went on vacation, when would you go? _____	d. I'd ask my teacher for more time.
5. If your friend was rude to you, what would you say? _____	e. I'd tell the principal.
6. What would you do if your family moved to a new city? _____	f. I'd tell her I was upset.

2 Circle the correct words.

Anna: Hey, David. What ¹**did / would** you do if your friend ²**asked / would ask** you to cheat on a test?

David: I'd say no! I'd never do that.

Anna: So, if your friend ³**cheated / would cheat**, who ⁴**did / would** you tell?

David: Hmm. I probably wouldn't tell anyone.

Anna: Really? Why ⁵**wouldn't / didn't** you tell anyone if your friend ⁶**did / would do** something wrong?

David: Well, I'd try to get my friend to do the right thing and tell someone.

Anna: That's a good idea.

3 Write the questions another way. Then answer the questions with your own information.

1. Where would you study if you had a test tomorrow?

Q: *If you had a test tomorrow, where would you study?*

A. *I'd study at the café.*

2. If you broke your friend's computer, what would you do?

Q: _____

A: _____

3. If you did someone a favor, who would you help?

Q: _____

A: _____

4. Where would you celebrate if you had a party for your birthday?

Q: _____

A: _____

5. What would you do if you didn't have homework tonight?

Q: _____

A: _____

4 Complete the questions. Use the pictures and answers to help you.

1. Q: What _____*would Tony do if it rained*_____?

A: He'd take an umbrella.

2. Q: Where _____?

A: They'd go rafting in Costa Rica.

3. Q: _____

A. She'd apologize to the teacher.

CONVERSATION Asking for and giving advice

1 Put the words in the correct order.

1. on / what's / going / ?

   What's going on?

2. advice / need / some / I / .

   _____

3. up / what's / sure / . / ?

   _____

4. do / what / I / should / ?

   _____

5. ask him / I / in person / you, / I'd / if / were / .

   _____

6. for it / you / asking him / have / tried / ?

   _____

2 Complete the conversation with the phrases from Exercise 1.

Haley:	Hi, Brian. You look upset. ¹ *What's going on?* _____
Brian:	Well, I'm really mad at Peter. I don't know what to do. ² _____
Haley:	³ _____
Brian:	Well, Peter borrowed my tablet last week, and he hasn't given it back. ⁴ _____
Haley:	⁵ _____
Brian:	Yes, I have. I sent him three text messages about it.
Haley:	You know, maybe he didn't read the texts. ⁶ _____
Brian:	Well, I guess that's a good idea.
Haley:	Yeah. You might be getting mad for no good reason!
Brian:	You're probably right. I'll go talk to him!

1 Complete the article with the imperative form of the verbs.

be	invite	not wait
✓ follow	join	remember
go	not be	

HOW TO MAKE FRIENDS

It can be difficult to make friends, especially if you move to a new city. So, how can you make friends easily?

1 _____Follow_____ this advice.

2 _____ places where there are a lot of teens. For example, go to a café or the library.

3 _____ a club. Do you like chess, sports, or photography? Find a club with your interests.

Find friends online with similar interests. But 4 _____ careful when you make friends online. Some people can be bullies online.

5 _____ to be friendly and smile when you meet new people. 6 _____ afraid to say hello and ask questions. 7 _____ for others to talk to you. You can be the one to start a conversation!

Stay in touch with new friends. Call, text, or email them.

8 _____ new friends to do things.

2 Read the article in Exercise 1 again. Circle the correct answers.

1. What's the title?
   a. Moving to a New City
   b. How to Make Friends
   c. Follow This Advice

2. What's the problem?
   a. Some people can be bullies online.
   b. It's hard to stay in touch with friends.
   c. It's sometimes hard to make friends.

3. Who does this problem affect?
   a. People who have moved to a new city.
   b. Teenagers who don't have any friends.
   c. People who want to make friends online.

4. What question does the article want to answer?
   a. Do you like making friends?
   b. How can you make friends easily?
   c. Why is it difficult to make friends?

3 Complete the article with the correct sentences.

Choose your friends carefully.
Don't be afraid to tell your friends they are wrong.
Get away from the situation.
✓ How can you avoid peer pressure?
Say "no" and mean it.

How to Avoid
PEER PRESSURE

Peer pressure is when your friends try to make you do things that they are doing. Sometimes, they might not be doing the right thing.

1 _____How can you avoid peer pressure?_____

Follow this advice.

2 _____

_____

It's important to be strong if you don't want to do something. You might have to say "no" more than once.

3 _____

_____

If you walk away from something you don't want to do, your friends can't make you do it.

4 _____

_____

Hang out with friends that make good decisions.

5 _____

_____

They may listen to you and decide to do the right thing.

1 Complete each sentence with a word or phrase from each box.

confused	bullying
embarrassing	clowns
interesting	✓ did me a favor
✓ surprised	do research
terrified	snakes
terrifying	wear a school uniform

1. I was _____surprised_____ when Rick
   ____did me a favor____. He never wants to help me.

2. I was _____ when the girls at school
   started _____ me. They were saying
   very mean things, and I was scared.

3. I think _____ are _____.
   I always scream when I see one outside in my
   yard.

4. I have to _____. I have to keep it on
   for my piano lesson because I don't have time to
   change. It's so _____!

5. I think it's _____ to
   _____.
   I love finding out about new things.

6. I'm _____. Sarah said she was
   afraid of _____, but she's posting
   pictures of them at the circus. It looks like she's
   having a good time.

2 Write the words in the correct places in the chart.

✓ elevators	relaxed
exhausted	the dark
getting extra credit	winning an award

Fears	*elevators*	
Feelings		
Rewards		

3 Complete the expressions with *do* or *make*.

1. ____*do*____ something fun

2. _____ me mad

3. _____ homework

4. _____ a difference

5. _____ friends

4 Look at the pictures. Complete the sentences with *be going to* and an expression from Exercise 3.

1. Isabel *is going to do something fun* this weekend.

2. Amy and Dan _____ at their
   new school.

3. You _____ if you don't clean
   your room.

4. Jeremy _____ after school.

5. I _____ in my community by
   helping others.

5 Circle the correct words.

1. Oh, no, you forgot to do your homework.
   You **can't /** (**must**) be really (**embarrassed**) /
   embarrassing.

2. This math problem is very **confused / confusing**.
   I think I **might / can't** have the wrong answer.

3. Ginger's vacation is **relaxed / relaxing**. She
   may / might not want to stay a few more days.

4. I'm **interested / interesting** in being a police
   officer, but it **must / must not** be very difficult.

5. Jen told me **surprised / surprising** news. She
   won an award. She **can't / might** be sad about
   that!

6. The race is going to be **exhausted / exhausting**.
   It **can't / could** take me an hour or more to finish.

6 Complete the conversations. Use *will* for decisions at the moment of speaking. Use the present continuous for planned events.

1. **A:** Do you want to go to a theme park this weekend?
   B: Sure. I _____*'ll go*_____ (go) with you.

2. **A:** What are you going to do tomorrow?
   B: I _____ (shop) with my sister.

3. **A:** When are you going to Lima?
   B: We _____ (fly) there tomorrow.

4. **A:** Do you have homework tonight?
   B: I _____ (not know) until after my next class.

5. **A:** How are you getting home?
   B: I'm not sure. I think I _____ (walk).

6. **A:** Where is your brother staying tonight?
   B: He _____ (sleep) at my grandparents' house.

7 Complete the sentences with the correct forms of the verbs.

1. If Jim didn't stay up so late, he _____*wouldn't feel*_____ (not feel) exhausted in the morning.

2. If Sara misses class again, she _____ (be) assigned detention.

3. If you _____ (not follow) the dress code, you'll be sent home.

4. If your best friend cheated on a test, what _____ you _____ (do)?

5. If Noah _____ (not be) rude, he wouldn't have to apologize.

6. If your classmates saw someone being bullied, _____ they _____ (tell) the teacher?

7. If you cheat on the test, you _____ (get) sent to the principal's office.

8. If you _____ (win) a prize, how would you feel?

9. If you are punctual, you _____ (not make) Mr. Gomez mad.

10. If you _____ (be) late to class, would you be embarrassed?

8 Complete the conversation.

Have you tried talking to him?	Come on!
Are you serious?	✓ I need some advice.
Sure. What's up?	What should I do?

Julia: Hey, Ryan.
¹ *I need some advice.* _____

Ryan: ² _____

Julia: Well, did you hear about Aaron? He was assigned to detention.

Ryan: ³ _____

Julia: Yes, I am. And he's not going to tell our parents.

Ryan: ⁴ _____
That doesn't sound like your brother.

Julia: I know.
⁵ _____

Ryan: ⁶ _____
You could tell him this: If he tells your parents before the principal does, it probably won't make them as mad.

Julia: That's a good idea.

7 *Smart* **Planet**

1 Find 10 more words for materials.

M	H	I	T	H	K	W	O	A	M	W	U	B	B	M
B	A	N	O	Z	O	J	T	L	E	N	N	G	R	P
R	U	B	B	E	R	U	I	C	T	U	I	S	P	Z
O	A	I	N	V	B	I	Y	B	A	A	Q	N	L	R
T	C	C	O	T	T	O	N	N	L	Y	A	T	A	T
O	K	E	A	I	L	I	P	L	A	N	T	S	S	I
E	P	M	I	Y	C	B	A	S	T	I	D	A	T	K
R	B	E	N	R	W	O	O	D	R	B	R	I	I	C
A	R	N	B	O	A	M	O	U	N	F	O	M	C	I
N	I	T	I	O	T	E	P	L	A	E	N	A	H	R
T	C	C	K	N	E	S	A	G	L	A	S	S	E	M
G	K	K	I	S	R	S	L	S	I	T	T	O	G	J
I	S	D	N	U	S	A	P	A	P	E	R	U	F	L

2 Cross out the word that doesn't belong to each category.

1. **Water:** ocean lake ~~mountain~~ river
2. **Wood:** house tablet guitar table
3. **Cement:** floor house road car
4. **Plants:** waterfall jungle rain forest farm
5. **Rubber:** tire T-shirt bath toy balloon
6. **Metal:** fork jewelry book chair
7. **Plastic:** magazine bottle keyboard cup
8. **Glass:** window mirror pottery light bulb

3 Complete the sentences with some of the materials from Exercise 1.

1. It's a ___cotton___ sweater.
2. I live in a _____ house.

3. It's a _____ jar.
4. I made a _____ airplane.

5. Do you like my new _____ boots?
6. Put those things in the _____ recycling bin.

7. _____ flows out of the fountain.
8. Use some _____ to start the fire.

4 Answer the questions with your own information.

1. What material is in the floors of your home?
   The floors in my home are wood.

2. What kind of bottle or can do you usually buy soda or juice in?
   _____

3. What kinds of clothes do you wear that are cotton?
   _____

4. What materials can you recycle in your area?
   _____

GRAMMAR Simple present passive; infinitives of purpose

1 Correct the sentences.

              is
1. My favorite T-shirt ~~are~~ made from cotton.

2. Those cars are built be less harmful to the environment.

3. The animals in the wildlife park isn't hunted.

4. The water on the river not frozen because it's not cold enough.

5. Rubber is used to made erasers.

6. Plastic bottles aren't recycle at our recycling center.

7. These plants grown in a greenhouse.

8. Water isn't sell in plastic bottles at that store.

2 Write sentences with the simple present passive.

1. the buildings / design / in California

   The buildings are designed in California.

2. the fruit / grow / in Mexico

   _____

3. the cabinets / not make / of wood

   _____

4. the wall / not paint / green

   _____

5. the park / clean / every weekend

   _____

6. the glass bottles / not reused / at the market

   _____

3 Look at the pictures and answer the questions.

1. Where is the house built?

   It's built in a forest.

2. What is the house made of?

   _____

3. What is recycled at the recycling center?

   _____

4. What isn't recycled?

   _____

5. Where are the oranges grown?

   _____

6. Where is the tomato sauce made?

   _____

4 Write sentences with the information in the chart. Use the simple present passive and infinitives of purpose.

What?	Why?
those cotton T-shirts / make	keep / people cool
that house / design	save / energy
plastic bottles / recycle	make / furniture
bricks / use	build / houses
that wood / save	make / fires

1. *Those cotton T-shirts are made to keep*

   people cool.

2. _____

3. _____

4. _____

5. _____

Eco-construction verbs

1 Circle seven more verbs.

abrichangetapgladiscoverplasavebuimakbuildtsyinodestrreducelcdfkcotdesignrtobbssconsumeduceinstallrplasttowrci

2 Put the words in the correct categories. Some words can go in more than one category. Then add one more idea for each category.

✓ a house	energy
a new plant	pollution
an air-conditioning unit	the rain forest
clothes	

Things you can . . .		Your ideas
1. build	*a house*	
2. change		
3. install		
4. reduce		
5. discover		
6. design	*a house*	
7. save		
8. consume		

3 Complete the sentences with the present continuous of the verbs from Exercise 1.

1. Mr. and Mrs. Henderson _are installing_ solar panels on their roof.

2. Jenny _____ money because she _____ her light bulbs to ones that don't use as much energy.

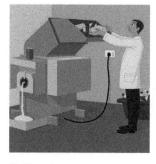

3. Tomás _____ a new way to recycle plastic.

4. Laura _____ a house for her parents.

5. They _____ a house in the city.

6. We _____ trash in our school by 50 percent.

GRAMMAR Simple past passive

1 Check (✓) if the sentences are active or passive.

	Active	Passive
1. The houses were built in 2013.		✓
2. The company installed three recycling bins in the cafeteria.		
3. John's family doesn't grow corn on their farm.		
4. Our windows weren't replaced after the last storm.		
5. Large amounts of fuel were consumed by cars and trucks last year.		
6. Sara designed three new eco-friendly homes this year.		

2 Circle the correct words.

○○○

Make your home or business work for you, and let Eco-Friendly Now help you.

● Last year, over 100 homes ¹**was made / were made** eco-friendly by our company.

● Two-hundred and fifty solar panels ²**installed / were installed** in local businesses. The businesses ³**saved / were saved** thousands of dollars on their electric bills.

● A new energy-saving technique ⁴**was developed / were developed** by our expert engineer. It ⁵**put / was put** in our first home last month.

● We ⁶**changed / were changed** air conditioning systems in 25 homes, and bills ⁷**reduced / were reduced** by 40 percent.

● Click here to read reviews that ⁸**was written / were written** by happy customers.

3 Complete the conversation with the simple past passive forms of the verbs.

Don: Hey, Kim. Are you going to join the School Improvement club?

Kim: What's that?

Don: Oh, it's a group at school that makes changes at our school. Last year, recycling bins ¹___*were put*___ (put) in the cafeteria by the group.

Kim: That's cool. What other things ²_____ (do) by the group?

Don: Well, 100 trees ³_____ (plant) around the school.

Eva: ⁴_____ the garden _____ (create) by the group, too?

Don: Yes, it ⁵_____. The garden ⁶_____ (design) by one of the group members.

Eva: ⁷_____ it _____ (design) by Julia Alvarez?

Don: No, it ⁸_____. I think the plans ⁹_____ (draw) by Mark Reynolds. Anyway, it's a great club.

Eva: How many people ¹⁰_____ (involve) in the group last year?

Don: About 10. But we're trying to get at least 25 members this year.

Eva: OK. I'll join!

4 Write simple past passive sentences and questions. Add *by* when needed.

1. my dress / make / my grandmother / .

   My dress was made by my grandmother.

2. our house / not build / a famous architect / .

   _____

3. the company / start / a designer / ?

   _____

4. those potatoes / not grow / local farmers / .

   _____

5. when / solar panels / invent / ?

   _____

6. the plastic bottles / recycle / the students / .

   _____

7. where / the pottery / find / ?

   _____

8. lights / leave on / the children / ?

   _____

CONVERSATION   Apologizing

1 Circle the correct words.

Ryan: This planting project was a great idea.

Carla: Yeah. The park is going to look so much better. Hey, Ryan, did you bring shovels for us?

Ryan: Oh, no. I forgot. I'm really ¹**sorry / fault**.

Carla: Ryan! How are we going to plant our trees? You said you'd bring them.

Ryan: I know. I didn't ²**forget / mean** to leave them at home.

Carla: Here comes Ms. Lee.

Ms. Lee: Hi, Carla and Ryan. What's going on? The other students have planted a lot of trees already.

Carla: My ³**sorry / apologies**. We forgot our shovels.

Ryan: It was my ⁴**fault / apologies**, Ms. Lee. I was supposed to bring the shovels, and I forgot.

Ms. Lee: Don't worry about it. You can borrow Javier's and Kayla's shovels. They're almost done.

2 Complete the conversation with the correct words.

apologies	fault	mean	sorry

Ana: Which flowers should we plant first?

Eric: Let's plant your flowers, Ana. Then we can plant Meg's. And finally mine. Meg, where are the flowers you brought?

Meg: Oh, I didn't bring any flowers. Was I supposed to?

Eric: We were all supposed to bring flowers.

Meg: Oh, I see. My ¹_____.

Eric: Now we don't have enough!

Meg: I didn't ²_____ to mess things up. I didn't know.

Eric: Well, the website about the planting project gave all of the information.

Ana: Eric, don't get mad at Meg. I invited her at the last minute. It was my ³_____. I forgot to tell her about the website, and I didn't tell her to bring flowers.

Eric: Oh, wow. I'm really ⁴_____, Meg.

Meg: That's OK. Hey, there's a garden center a few minutes away. I'll go buy some flowers now.

Eric: No! I'll go get them, Meg.

Ana: Hey, let's plant these flowers first, and then we'll all go!

1 **Read the article. Then match the words to different words that refer to the same thing.**

Riverdale Teens Have An
Animal Adoption Day

by Jordan Pierce

Fifteen Riverdale High School students found homes for animals on Saturday, May 6. The teens worked with the Riverdale Animal Shelter to find homes for cats and dogs. They organized an Animal Adoption Day. They got 20 cats and dogs from the shelter and took them to Riverdale Park for the event. They set up a table there with signs and information about the animals.

All 20 animals were adopted by Riverdale families. The shelter was very happy with the results. It is going to continue working with the teenagers and have an Animal Adoption Day once a month.

1. Riverdale High School students __c__, _____, _____

2. animals _____, _____

3. the Riverdale Animal Shelter _____, _____

4. Animal Adoption Day _____

5. Riverdale Park _____

a. cats and dogs

b. the event

c. they

d. it

e. the teens

f. there

g. the teenagers

h. them

i. the shelter

2 **Read the article in Exercise 1 again. Answer the questions.**

1. What was the event?

   The event was an Animal Adoption Day.

2. When was it?

   _____

3. Where was it?

   _____

4. Who was involved?

   _____

5. What did they do?

   _____

6. What were the results?

   _____

7. What will happen next?

   _____

8 Run for Cover!

VOCABULARY Natural disasters

1 Put the letters in the correct order to make words.

1. O N T R O A D   _tornado_
2. D D L L I N A E S   _____
3. M S A T I N U   _____
4. R N H U I A C E R   _____
5. C N C O V L A I   _____
6. E T R F O S   _____
7. O L F O D   _____
8. U A T A E Q K E R H   _____
9. O R E P N U I T   _____
10. I F E R   _____
11. A A C E V A L N H   _____

2 Label the pictures with the correct words from Exercise 1.

1. _tornado_

2. _____

3. _____

4. _____

5. _____

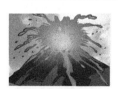

6. _____

7. _____

8. _____

9. _____

3 Where do the natural disasters happen? Write the words in the correct places in the chart. Some words can go in more than one category.

✓ avalanche	forest fire	tornado
earthquake	hurricane	tsunami
flood	landslide	volcanic eruption

On land	In the air	In the ocean
avalanche		

4 When do the natural disasters happen? Check (✓) the answers that are true for your area. Then answer the questions.

	Often	Sometimes	Never
1. avalanches			
2. earthquakes			
3. floods			
4. forest fires			
5. hurricanes			
6. landslides			
7. tornadoes			
8. tsunamis			
9. volcanic eruptions			

1. Which natural disasters happen most often in your area?

   In my area, tornadoes happen most often.

   _____

2. Which natural disasters never happen in your area? Have you ever experienced them in other places?

   _____

   _____

GRAMMAR Past perfect

1 Write the past perfect forms of the verbs.

1. plan _had planned_

2. be _____

3. not be _____

4. ski _____

5. not finish _____

6. not see _____

7. hear _____

8. feel _____

2 Complete the paragraph with verbs from Exercise 1.

○○○

Tell us your NATURAL DISASTER STORIES

Rachel Patterson:

My family [1] _had planned_ a trip to Japan. Then we couldn't go because my father got sick. We finally went a year later. We [2] _____ there for two days when an earthquake happened. I [3] _____ earthquakes in California before, but never one like this! We were at a restaurant, and I [4] _____ my lunch. It went flying across the room!

David Alba:

I [5] _____ snow before. But last week, I saw a lot of it! I went skiing in Denver, Colorado. I took ski lessons on the first day. My instructor [6] _____ all over the world, and she was a great teacher.

There [7] _____ an avalanche at the ski resort in over 10 years. However, on the second day, my instructor [8] _____ on TV that conditions were right for avalanches, so she cancelled our lessons. Later that day, no one was allowed to ski, and there was an avalanche! Luckily, I was safe!

3 Read the sentences. Then circle the answer that correctly explains each situation.

1. Elsa hadn't been to Costa Rica before her trip.

   a. She has been to Costa Rica more than once.

   b. She went to Costa Rica once.

2. The forest fire had started before breakfast.

   a. The forest fire started in the morning.

   b. The forest fire started in the afternoon.

3. Andrew had read an interesting article about tsunamis.

   a. Andrew read an article about tsunamis.

   b. Andrew didn't read an article about tsunamis.

4. Sun-hi hadn't told Paul about the hurricane.

   a. Paul knew about the hurricane.

   b. Paul didn't know about the hurricane.

5. June had finished the reading before school.

   a. June finished the reading.

   b. June didn't finish the reading.

6. The weather hadn't been good before the disaster.

   a. The disaster caused the weather to be bad.

   b. The disaster didn't cause the weather to be bad.

Past perfect *yes/no* questions

4 Write yes/no questions and answers in the past perfect. ✓ = yes, ✗ = no.

1. Dylan / hear / about the volcanic eruption / (✗)

   Q: _Had Dylan heard about the volcanic eruption?_

   A: _No, he hadn't._

2. you / be / to San Francisco before the earthquake / (✓)

   Q: _____

   A: _____

3. Sally / read / the article before class / (✗)

   Q: _____

   A: _____

4. your parents / tell / about the flood / (✗)

   Q: _____

   A: _____

5. the volcano / be / quiet for several months (✓)

   Q: _____

   A: _____

6. you and your brother / see / a tornado / before / (✓)

   Q: _____

   A: _____

VOCABULARY Survival essentials

1 Match the sentences to the pictures.

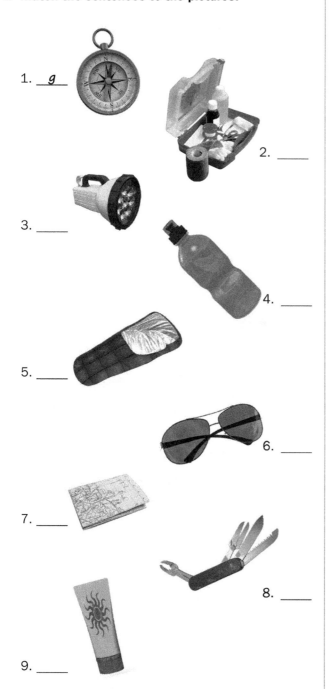

1. _g_

2. ____

3. ____

4. ____

5. ____

6. ____

7. ____

8. ____

9. ____

a. I always take a water bottle when I hike.

b. A penknife is useful on a camping trip.

c. You should wear sunglasses when it's sunny.

d. You should always wear sunscreen outside.

e. I cut my finger. I need a first-aid kit.

f. Your sleeping bag looks really warm.

g. Which way is north? Do you have a compass?

h. I need a flashlight. I'm afraid of the dark!

i. John had forgotten to bring a map on the hike.

2 Read the situations and circle the correct answers.

1. Gabriel is skiing in the mountains. It's really bright outside. What does he need?

   a. a compass   b. a first-aid kit   c. sunscreen

2. Carol is lost in a forest. She wants to find her way out before it's dark. What should she use?

   a. a penknife   b. a compass   c. a flashlight

3. Han is camping and sleeping in a tent. What does he need to stay warm?

   a. a flashlight   b. a sleeping bag   c. sunglasses

4. Mara fell and hurt her foot while snowboarding. What does she need?

   a. a water bottle   b. a penknife   c. a first-aid kit

5. Dan and Ethan need to cut a rope on their tent. What should they use?

   a. a penknife   b. sunscreen   c. a first-aid kit

6. Yae-won needs directions to the campgrounds. What should she use?

   a. a sleeping bag   b. a compass   c. a map

3 Answer the questions with words from Exercise 1.

1. Which two items protect you from the sun?

   _____

   _____

2. Which two items help you with directions?

   _____

   _____

3. Which two items would you most likely use at night?

   _____

   _____

4. Which two items would you most likely use for food or drink?

   _____

   _____

GRAMMAR Past perfect and simple past

1 Look at the timeline of Carl's trip. Complete the sentences with the past perfect or simple past. Use the past perfect for the event that happened first in each sentence.

9 a.m.

pack his bags

forget his sleeping bag

leave for trip

go fishing

set up tent

friends arrive

start a fire

cook the fish

everyone eat

go to bed

10 p.m.

1. Carl ____had packed____ had packed his bags a week before he _____left_____ for his trip.

2. He _____ fishing before he _____ his tent.

3. He _____ his tent already when his friends _____ at the campsite.

4. A few minutes before Carl _____ the fish, he _____ a fire.

5. Everyone _____ a delicious fish dinner a few hours before they _____ to bed.

6. When Carl _____ to bed, he realized that he _____ his sleeping bag!

2 Circle the correct words. Use the past perfect for the event that happened first in each sentence.

1. On a long hike, John **dropped /** **had dropped** his compass 20 minutes before he **realized** **/ had realized** it.

2. My sister **heard / had heard** about the hurricane before I **told / had told** her about it.

3. I **cut / had cut** my finger making dinner, and unfortunately, I **didn't buy / hadn't bought** a first-aid kit.

4. Sam and Jill were hungry on their hike because they **didn't pack / hadn't packed** any snacks before they **left / had left**.

5. When they **rescued / had rescued** the hikers, they **were / had been** lost for two days.

6. I was upset because after I **bought / had bought** my penknife, the store **had / had had** a big sale.

3 Write sentences with the simple past and past perfect. Use the past perfect for the event that happened first in each sentence.

1. Jessica / sign up / for a camping trip / after / her friend / tell her about it

   Jessica signed up for the camping trip

   after her friend had told her about it.

2. By the time / Raul / buy / his bike, / he / save / money for two months

   _____

   _____

3. I / not check / the weather report / before / I / go / hiking

   _____

   _____

4. We / pack / our suitcase / a week before / we / leave

   _____

   _____

5. Serena / not hear / about the tsunami / before / she / talk / to her brother

   _____

   _____

6. After / the news / be / on for an hour, / I / finally / hear / the weather report

   _____

   _____

1 Circle the correct words.

1. Oh, **no** / **know**!

2. I don't **think** / **know** what to do!

3. Let me **think** / **panic**.

4. What's the **matter** / **wrong**?

5. **No** / **Don't** panic.

2 Complete the conversation with the expressions from Exercise 1.

Mae: Hey, Joe. What direction are we going in?

Joe: 1 _____*Oh, no!*_____ I don't believe this!

Mae: 2 _____

Joe: I can't find my compass! This is terrible!

Mae: 3 _____ Let's think about this calmly. When did you have it last?

Joe: 4 _____ Oh, I remember. I took it out of my bag at the beginning of the hike. I must have dropped it.

Mae: Well, it's no big deal. We can use the sun to see what direction we're going.

Joe: I know, but my grandfather had given me that compass before he moved to California. It's really special. 5 _____

Mae: Oh, now I see why you're so upset. Listen, we've only been hiking for 20 minutes. Let's go back and see if we can find it.

Joe: That'd be great. Thanks, Mae.

READING TO WRITE

1 **Complete Kyle's story with the adverb form of the words in parentheses.**

I'll never forget Friday, April 17. I was at my friend's house in the morning. We didn't have school that day because of high winds and heavy rain. I had heard on the news we might have a flood in our town, and ¹ _unfortunately_ (unfortunate), we did. The water was so high that our street was like a river. By noon, the rain had stopped, so my friend and I played in the street. ² _____ (natural), we thought it was fun. We didn't realize how bad things were. The water kept rising. ³ _____ (sudden), my parents showed up at my friend's house. They were really worried. They had left work early and said we had to go home ⁴ _____ (immediate). ⁵ _____ (fortunate), our house was OK, but many homes were destroyed. I felt terrible. On Saturday, I volunteered in my neighborhood to clean up the streets.

2 **Read the article in Exercise 1 again. Circle the correct answers.**

1. What happened?

    a. A hurricane destroyed many homes.

    b. There was a flood, but no homes were destroyed.

    c. There was a flood, and homes were destroyed.

2. When did it happen?

    a. On Friday, April 17

    b. On Saturday, April 17

    c. On Saturday, April 18

3. Where was Kyle when it happened?

    a. At home

    b. At a friend's house

    c. At school

4. How did Kyle feel about the flood?

    a. At first he thought it was fun, and then he felt bad.

    b. At first he felt bad, but then he thought it was fun.

    c. At first he felt terrible, and then he got really worried.

5. What happened at the end of the story?

    a. Kyle played in the water.

    b. Kyle helped clean up the streets.

    c. Kyle's parents took him home.

3 **Complete Brianna's story with the correct sentences.**

> Fortunately, there wasn't really an avalanche.
> I was really embarrassed.
> In the end, it turned out OK.
> ✓ Last Saturday was a terrible day.
> Suddenly, my sister shouted, "Avalanche!"
> Unfortunately, I broke Tara's snowboard.

○○○

¹ _Last Saturday was a terrible day._

I went snowboarding on a mountain near my town.

My friend Tara let me borrow her snowboard.

² _____

I got really scared, and I ran into a tree.

³ _____

My sister was joking.

⁴ _____

The snowboard hit the tree when I ran into it, and it cracked. I called Tara that night to tell her.

⁵ _____

Snowboards are expensive, and I didn't have enough money to buy her a new one.

⁶ _____

My sister felt terrible about her joke, so she gave me money to buy Tara a new board!

1 Write the words in the correct places in the chart.

✓ cement forest fire plants
compass hurricane rubber
first aid kit metal tsunami
flashlight penknife volcanic eruption

Materials	Survival essentials	Natural disasters
cement	_____	_____
_____	_____	_____
_____	_____	_____
_____	_____	_____

2 Look at the pictures and complete the puzzle. Find out what the city did by filling in the gray boxes.

The city _____ their trash last year by 50 percent.

```
       1 t o r n a d o
    2 □ □ □ □ □ □ □
  3 □ □ □ □ □ □
         4 □ □ □ □ □ □
5 □ □ □ □ □ □
       6 □ □ □ □ □ □ □
       7 □ □ □ □ □
```

1.

2.

3.

4.

5.

6.

7.

3 Complete each sentence with a word from each box. Use the simple present passive forms of the verbs.

build	bricks
design	cotton
make	glass
recycle	paper
turn	✓ plastic
✓ use	water

1. ___*Plastic is used*___ to make this jewelry.

2. These shirts _____ of _____.

3. _____ bags _____ to help the environment.

4. This house _____ with _____.

5. The _____ lamps _____ by an artist.

6. The wheel _____ by _____.

4 **Put the words in the correct order to make sentences. Change the verbs to the simple past passive.**

1. by / the solar panels / install / an engineer / .

   The solar panels were installed by an engineer.

2. the flood / save / after / our dog / .

   _____

3. build / when / the house / ?

   _____

4. not discover / right away / the forest fire / .

   _____

5. little energy / the EcoHouse / by / consume / .

   _____

6. by / invent / an American / solar panels / ?

   _____

5 **Correct the conversations. Use the past perfect.**

1. **A:** Had you ~~hear~~ *heard* about the flood before the class?

   B: Yes, I ~~have~~ *had*.

2. **A:** What has you learned about Brazil before your trip?

   B: I had reading a lot about the food there.

3. **A:** Had Jake call you before he came over?

   B: No, he not.

4. **A:** Were Tom and Keiko been on a boat before their cruise?

   B: No, they haven't.

5. **A:** Where has you worked before you got this job?

   B: I had no worked anywhere. This is my first job.

6. **A:** Had you help on a volunteer project before?

   B: Yes, I hadn't.

7. **A:** What had happen before the flood?

   B: It has rained for several days.

8. **A:** Has you known about the tsunami before you went there?

   B: No, I not.

6 **Complete the article with the simple past or past perfect forms of the verbs.**

Samantha and her friend Lydia ¹_____*went*_____ (go) on a hike last Saturday. Samantha ²_____ (not be) in a forest before the trip, but Lydia ³_____ (go) many times. Lydia ⁴_____ (tell) Samantha about the forest before they ⁵_____ (get) there. Samantha ⁶_____ (not ask) Lydia what to bring before she ⁷_____ (pack) her bag for the trip. She ⁸_____ (take) a lot of water, some snacks, and her camera. On the hike, they ⁹_____ (walk) for about an hour when Samantha ¹⁰_____ (fall) and ¹¹_____ (cut) her knee. Unfortunately, Samantha ¹²_____ (not pack) a first-aid kit before they ¹³_____ (leave) for the hike, but, fortunately, Lydia had!

7 **Complete the conversation.**

Don't panic	I didn't mean to
I don't know what to do	I'm really sorry
Let me think	✓ What's the matter?

Rob: You look terrible. ¹____*What's the matter?*____

Ian: I'm really worried about the hurricane.

Rob: ²_____. The news said it probably won't be that bad.

Ian: No, I don't mean the hurricane here. I'm worried about the hurricane that hit Mexico. My grandparents live there.

Rob: Oh, ³_____ be rude. Now I see what you mean. ⁴_____.

Ian: That's OK. It's just that they aren't answering their phones, and ⁵_____.

Rob: Do you have the number for any of their neighbors?

Ian: Hmm . . . ⁶_____. Yes, my cousins live close by. I'll text them now. Thanks.

9 He Said, She Said

VOCABULARY Reporting verbs

1 Find nine more reporting verbs.

B	I	L	T	Z	J	O	G	V	A	Y	I	W
S	A	Y	P	N	B	P	R	O	M	N	S	H
O	N	I	S	U	G	G	E	S	T	A	T	I
G	N	U	W	I	S	Z	K	H	D	Y	N	S
G	O	U	P	U	S	T	L	O	P	G	E	P
E	U	F	R	Y	C	B	Q	U	A	G	M	E
R	N	S	O	R	H	I	L	T	R	B	A	R
G	C	O	M	P	L	A	I	N	E	F	N	M
P	E	Y	I	X	D	E	P	C	N	E	V	A
L	H	W	S	N	X	T	E	L	L	M	I	T
A	V	K	E	S	O	S	L	E	R	P	B	E
I	J	X	K	T	E	X	P	L	A	I	N	O
Y	R	E	M	I	N	D	L	A	N	N	G	P

2 Circle the correct words.

1. Jennifer **said** / **reminded** she did well on her science test.

2. My dad **whispered** / **promised** me he'd drive us to the concert.

3. Who **suggested** / **announced** that we eat at this restaurant? It's great.

4. My brother always **explains** / **complains** about doing his chores.

5. Can you **promise** / **remind** me when our homework is due?

6. Diego **suggested** / **told** me about his vacation.

7. Please **whisper** / **shout** in the library. Talking loudly bothers people who are reading.

8. Lydia **told** / **explained** the computer program to us.

9. Tyrone **announced** / **said** his plans to get a summer job.

10. Maria was so surprised by a text message that she **shouted** / **told** in the middle of a store.

3 Complete the sentences with the simple past form of some of the verbs from Exercise 1.

1. During the game last week, the coach _____*shouted*_____ loudly at the players, but they couldn't hear him.

2. I _____ my best friend that I would text her when I got home.

3. My brother _____ when it was his turn to take out the trash.

4. Yesterday Kai _____ to me that we should meet after class.

5. At the assembly, the principal _____ the winner of the class prize.

6. Mr. Sato _____ the assignment to us twice, because it was a little confusing.

4 Complete the sentences with your own information.

1. I usually whisper _*when I'm talking in the library*_ .

2. I often have to explain things to _____.

3. When I complain, I usually complain about _____.

4. _____ sometimes has to remind me to _____.

5. People often shout when _____.

6. One time, _____ promised me _____.

GRAMMAR Quoted speech vs. reported speech

1 Add commas and quotation marks to the direct speech sentences in the correct places.

1. Veronica said, "I was really tired yesterday."

2. I've seen that movie John announced.

3. We'll come to your party they told us.

4. Mr. Valdez shouted You can't run in the hallway!

5. Sam whispered It's dark in here.

2 Match the quoted speech sentences to the reported speech sentences. Use one reported speech sentence twice.

1. Maya said, "I won't call them." __d__	a. Maya said that she called them every day.
2. Maya said, "I'm calling them right now." _____	b. Maya said that she had called them.
3. Maya said, "I called them." _____	c. Maya said that she had been calling them.
4. Maya said, "I've called them." _____	d. Maya said that she wouldn't call them.
5. Maya said, "I call them every day." _____	e. Maya said that she was calling them right now.
6. Maya said, "I was calling them." _____	

3 Put the words in the correct order to make reported speech sentences.

1. was / explained / sick the day of the party / that she / Emily

   Emily explained that she was sick the day

   of the party.

2. could / me / chess / that he / Hiro / play / told

   _____

3. had / I / been / said / to Ecuador / I / that

   _____

4. was / Shelby / that she / complained / tired

   _____

5. that he / moved / Mike / had / announced /

   _____

6. said / soccer / played / that she / Alba

   _____

4 Complete the direct and quoted speech sentences with the correct forms of the verbs.

1. "It ___looks___ stormy outside," Luisa said.

   She said that it looked stormy outside.

2. "I walk my dog every day," Greg said.

   He said that he _____ his dog every day.

3. "I'll call you," Marissa told me.

   She told me that she _____ me.

4. "I _____ you," Sarah explained.

   She explained that she could help me.

5. "I _____ at the park," Nidia said.

   She said that she had been skateboarding in the park.

6. "Ling bought a new jacket," Dan said.

   He said that Ling _____ a new jacket.

5 Write the quotes from a website as reported speech.

```
○○○
```

1. **Katie:** I just read a great book. ☺

   Katie said that she had just read a great book.

2. **Mario:** I studied all night last night. ☹

   _____

   _____

3. **Nora:** I'll post photos of the party soon. ☺

   _____

   _____

4. **Mia:** I can go to the soccer game on Friday! ☺

   _____

   _____

5. **Peter:** I've lost my keys. ☹

   _____

   _____

6. **Carol:** I'm ready for vacation. ☀

   _____

   _____

7. **Ted:** My cousins will be in town tomorrow! ☺

   _____

   _____

8. **Bert:** I went to a great concert on Saturday. ♪

   _____

   _____

VOCABULARY Communication methods

1 Fill in the letters to complete the words.

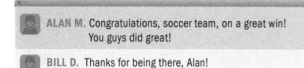

ALAN M. Congratulations, soccer team, on a great win! You guys did great!

BILL D. Thanks for being there, Alan!

1. s <u>o</u> <u>c</u> <u>i</u> <u>a</u> l n <u>e</u> t w o <u>r</u> <u>k</u> p <u>o</u> <u>s</u> <u>t</u>

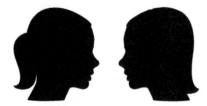

2. c _ _ _ t _ _ g

Tonya's Recipe of the Day
Pumpkin Cake   **October 3**

I know you all are going to love this recipe! It has so . . .

3. b _ _ _ _ _ _ t

4. v _ _ e _ _ h _ t

5. _ _ x _ m _ _ _ a g _

Today's discussion:
Which apps are the best for photography?

6. f _ r _ _

7. _ h _ _ e _ a _ l

HeartMusic04
Best concert ever! See the live video here:
http://cupurl/concert

8. _ _ _ _ r o _ _ o _ p _ s _

From: Marci
To: Penny
Cc:
Subject: When can you go out ?

9. e _ _ i _

2 Write the words from Exercise 1 next to their definitions.

1. A message you put on a social networking page:
   social network post

2. Talking and seeing video of someone computer to computer: _____

3. An online discussion with several people:
   _____

4. Talking with others in an informal way:
   _____

5. A way to communicate with someone using only your voice (you can't see the other person):
   _____

6. A message you send to someone over the Internet that contains a subject line:
   _____

7. Personal writing on a website that usually shares an experience or opinion and which is usually added to often: _____

8. A short note you type on your phone and send to someone: _____

9. A very short message on a social networking page: _____

3 Check (✓) how often you do these things.

	Often	Sometimes	Never
1. I video chat with my friends or family.			
2. I chat with friends after school.			
3. I make phone calls.			
4. I write social network posts about my day.			
5. I join online forums.			
6. I send my friends text messages.			

Reported questions

1 Match the direct questions with the reported questions.

1. "When do you eat dinner?" he asked. _d_	a. He asked me if I had eaten dinner.
2. "When did you eat dinner?" he asked. ___	b. He asked me when I had eaten dinner.
3. "When will you eat dinner?" he asked. ___	c. He asked me when I could eat dinner.
4. "When can you eat dinner?" he asked. ___	d. He asked me when I ate dinner.
5. "Did you eat dinner?" he asked. ___	e. He asked me when I would eat dinner.

2 Correct the reported questions.

1. "Why are you tired?" Sandra asked.
   why
   Sandra asked me ~~if~~ I was tired.

2. Haru asked, "Who is your teacher?"
   Haru asked me who was my teacher.

3. Marcos asked, "What have you done today?"
   Marcos asked me what I have done today.

4. "Which sweater did you like?" Trisha asked.
   Trisha asked me which sweater had I liked.

5. Ahmed asked, "Can you help me?"
   Ahmed asked me when I could help him.

6. "Will you come to my party?" Anne asked.
   Anne asked me if I came to her party.

7. "Have you been online today?" asked my mom.
   My mom asked if I am been online today.

8. Dana asked, "Did you do your homework tonight?"
   Dana asked if we had been doing our homework tonight.

3 Write the questions as reported speech.

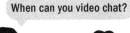

 Dan Wendy

1. *Dan asked Wendy when she could video chat.*

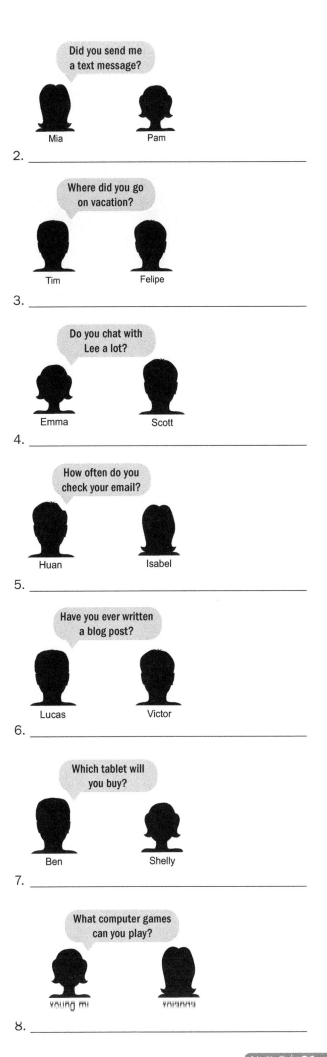

Did you send me a text message?

Mia   Pam

2. _____

Where did you go on vacation?

Tim   Felipe

3. _____

Do you chat with Lee a lot?

Emma   Scott

4. _____

How often do you check your email?

Huan   Isabel

5. _____

Have you ever written a blog post?

Lucas   Victor

6. _____

Which tablet will you buy?

Ben   Shelly

7. _____

What computer games can you play?

Young mi   Yolanda

8. _____

1 Put the words in the correct order to make sentences.

1. what / definitely / happened / that's / not / .

   That's definitely not what happened.

2. that Tina had cheated / had happened, / I asked Kyle / what / and he said / .

   _____

   _____

3. I / that's / what / heard / not / !

   _____

   _____

4. to detention / was assigned / Kyle / according to Jen, / .

   _____

   _____

5. with / you / how / come up / that idea / did / ?

   _____

   _____

6. had posted it / Ricardo said / online yesterday / that Kyle / well, / .

   _____

   _____

2 Complete the conversation with the expressions from Exercise 1.

Lola: We're going to have a great soccer team this year.

Gabe: I know. Kyle is going to be the team captain.

Lola: He is? [1]*How did you come up with that idea?*

Gabe: [2]_____

His post said, "I'm so excited to be our soccer team's captain. Go Rangers!"

Lola: Hmm. I don't know about that.
[3]_____

She said that he couldn't be captain now. He might not even be able to play on the team because he cheated on a test.

Gabe: [4]_____

Lola: Really? How do you know it didn't happen?

Gabe: [5]_____

She looked at his answers during the test, but he didn't do anything wrong.

Lola: [6]_____!
I heard that *he* cheated off Tina.

Gabe: I don't think so. Hey, here comes Tina now. Let's ask her what happened.

READING TO WRITE

1 Complete Leo's essay with the correct words.

For paragraph 2:

| also | in addition | ✓ for one thing |

For paragraph 3:

| first | finally | in addition |

○○○

ONLINE RESEARCH
by Leo Rodriguez

1 Are you like most students? Do you use the Internet for school projects and homework? Doing research online can be easy, but it can also have its share of problems.

2 Online research is extremely convenient. [1] *For one thing*, it can be done at school, in the library, or at home. One writer says that a benefit of online research is that the Internet is available 24 hours a day. It is [2]_____ easy to find information on any topic you can imagine, simply by searching for your topic with key words. [3]_____, you can find many kinds of sources online, like newspaper and magazine articles, forums, blogs, and science reports.

3 Although it's convenient, there can be problems with online research. [4]_____, anyone can post information online, and this information isn't always true. [5]_____, research can be dated, meaning it was posted years ago, and it may not be true anymore. [6]_____, some good sources, like magazines, might require you to pay to read them.

4 I believe that doing research online is the best way to research because it's convenient and there is information available on any topic. However, I think people need to be careful. Check facts on several sites to be sure the information is true and check the dates on articles on websites. If used correctly, online research can be a great way to get information about a topic.

2 Read the article in Exercise 1 again. Write the paragraph numbers next to each section below.

_____ A paragraph with arguments against

_____ A conclusion

_____ An introduction

_____ A paragraph with arguments in favor

3 Read the article in Exercise 1 again. Answer the questions.

1. What does Leo use to get the reader's attention?
   _____

2. What reasons does Leo give in favor of online research?
   _____
   _____
   _____

3. What reasons does he give against online research?
   _____
   _____
   _____

4. Overall, does Leo think doing research online is a good idea or a bad one?
   _____

5. What two things does he think people can do to avoid problems with online research?
   _____
   _____

10 Don't Give Up!

VOCABULARY Goals and achievements

1 Put the letters in the correct order to make words about goals and achievements.

1. L E D A   I H T W   _deal with_

2. K L I S L   _____

3. E A F C   _____

4. A L G O   _____

5. E D A R R W   _____

6. R S G E R P S O   _____

7. C R E M P N E F R O A   _____

8. L E H A G C E L N   _____

9. I A E H C E V   _____

10. T T C N M M I O M E   _____

2 Circle the correct words.

1. Josh **challenged / achieved** his goal of running 5 kilometers in under 30 minutes.

2. How do you usually **deal with / reward** difficult problems?

3. Rita made **progress / goal** over the weekend on her school project.

4. Taking care of a pet is a **big commitment / skill**.

5. Everyone has to **achieve / face** challenges in life.

6. Playing the piano well takes **performance / skill** and practice.

7. Aimi's tennis coach **deals with / challenges** her with difficult tasks.

8. Raul's **progress / performance** at the concert was amazing.

9. The winner of the contest is **faced / rewarded** with $1,000.

10. I reached my **goal / commitment** of getting 100 percent on a math test.

3 Complete the questions with some of the words from Exercise 1. Then circle the answers that are true for you.

1. How do you usually ____ _deal with_ ____ challenges?

   a. I face them right away.

   b. I ask friends for their opinions and then face the challenge on my own.

   c. I ask friends and family to help me face challenges.

2. How do you feel about giving a _____ in front of people?

   a. I love it!

   b. It makes me nervous, but I enjoy the challenge.

   c. I hate it!

3. Who or what do you have the biggest _____ to in your life right now?

   a. a friend or family member

   b. a pet

   c. a class or job

4. Which _____ are you best at?

   a. playing a musical instrument

   b. playing a sport

   c. using a computer program

5. Which _____ would you most like to reach?

   a. buying a house or a car

   b. getting a job

   c. finishing school

6. If you won a contest, which _____ would you most like to get?

   a. money

   b. a bicycle or car

   c. a trip to another country

1 Write the correct reflexive pronoun for each subject.

Subject pronoun	Reflexive pronoun
1. I	*myself*
2. you	/ yourselves
3. he	
4. she	
5. we	
6. they	

2 Complete the paragraphs with reflexive pronouns from Exercise 1.

Hard Work and Rewards

When you work hard, you should reward ¹ _____yourself_____ ! Look at these examples of how people rewarded

² _____ for their hard work.

Sheila spent hours studying for a big math test. She passed the test. After the test, she went to the mall and bought

³ _____ a new phone.

Andrew trained for a 5-kilometer race. For several weeks, he only ate healthy food. After the race, he treated

⁴ _____ to a burger and French fries.

Liv and Rachel wanted to learn Spanish. Liv says, "We decided to teach ⁵ _____ Spanish instead of taking a class." They spent months learning Spanish together. As a reward, they took a trip to Mexico.

Feng wanted to learn to ski in a weekend. He went on a ski trip, took lessons, and got pretty good. He says, "I set a challenging goal for ⁶ _____ , and I achieved it!" As a reward, he bought some new skis.

Reflexive pronouns with *by*

3 Rewrite the sentences. Add *by* and the correct reflexive pronoun.

1. My little brother can ride a bike.

   My little brother can ride a bike by himself.

2. Can you make dinner?

   _____

3. Anna likes to travel.

   _____

4. We painted our room.

   _____

5. I learned to play the guitar.

   _____

6. Kim and Ed dealt with the problem.

   _____

4 Answer the questions with your own information.

1. What is something you like to do by yourself?

   I like to go to the movies by myself.

2. What is something young children usually can't do by themselves?

   _____

   _____

3. What kinds of things do you usually buy for yourself?

   _____

   _____

4. What is something that people can teach themselves?

   _____

   _____

5. What goals have you set for yourself?

   _____

   _____

6. Do you ever talk to yourself? When?

   _____

   _____

VOCABULARY Emotions related to accomplishments

1 Look at the pictures and complete the crossword.

¹e	x	²c	i	t	e	³d					

ACROSS

1.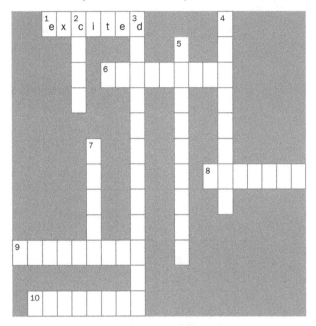

6.

8.

9.

10.

DOWN

2.

3.

4.

5.

7.

2 Circle the correct words.

1. My sister learned how to program computers by herself. I'm very **satisfied / proud / prepared /** of her.

2. Rafael was **miserable / confident /** thrilled that his soccer team won first place.

3. Miya was **nervous / disappointed / calm** before the performance, but she did a great job.

4. I studied a lot and was **excited / prepared / proud** for the test, but it was still difficult.

5. Do you get **excited / miserable / calm** when you get rewarded for something?

6. Farah was **nervous / disappointed / satisfied** that she didn't get a part in the school play.

7. We were **thrilled / miserable / confident** on our ski trip because there wasn't any snow.

8. Are you **proud / prepared / satisfied** with your test score, or do you think you could have done better?

9. I'm **confident / disappointed / nervous** that Jenna is going to win the race. I'll be so happy for her.

10. You are always so **excited / calm / thrilled** before a presentation. Why don't you get nervous?

3 Answer the questions with words from Exercise 1.

1. How do you feel before a test?

   I feel nervous, but if I study, I also feel prepared!

2. How do you feel when you achieve a goal?

   _____

   _____

3. How do you feel when you don't achieve a goal?

   _____

   _____

4. How do you feel before a trip?

   _____

   _____

GRAMMAR Causative *have/get*

1 Read the sentences. Then circle the answer that correctly explains each situation.

1. Joanna took a picture of herself.

   (a. Joanna took her own picture.)

   b. Another person took Joanna's picture.

2. My father has his shirts cleaned every week.

   a. My father cleans his own shirts.

   b. Another person cleans my father's shirts.

3. Terrance got his bicycle fixed.

   a. Terrance fixed his own bike.

   b. Another person fixed Terrance's bike.

4. I usually cut my hair myself.

   a. I cut my own hair.

   b. Another person cuts my hair.

5. Sandra gets her phone updated at TechService.

   a. Sandra updates her phone herself.

   b. Another person updates Sandra's phone.

2 Correct the sentences.

1. I ~~gotten~~ *get* my teeth cleaned twice a year.

2. We had our TV fix at Electric City.

3. Hyo's soccer team had their picture took.

4. Has Linda got her eyes checked?

5. Mr. and Mrs. Simone have had food made for Katy's party last year.

6. Carlos is getting his hair cutting.

3 Put the words in the correct order to make sentences.

1. her skateboard / got / last week / Lilly / fixed

   Lilly got her skateboard fixed last week.

2. delivered / had / we / to our mother / flowers

   _____

3. had gotten / Max / cut / for the picture / his hair

   _____

4. once a year / checked / get / my bicycle / I

   _____

5. his snowboard / painted / red and black / Jack / had

   _____

4 Complete the sentences about what the people got or had done with the correct words. Use the simple past of *have/get*.

get / her car / wash	have / her eyes / check
✓ get / her hair / do	have / his tablet / fix
get / his elbow / examine	have / their dog / clean

1. Mary _____ *got her hair done* _____ yesterday.

2. Brandon _____ last week.

3. Teresa and Leo _____ on Saturday.

4. Linh _____ last night.

5. Paul _____ on Monday.

6. Janet _____ last month.

CONVERSATION Reassuring someone

1 Match the phrases to make sentences.

1. You've faced _____   a. help you.

2. I think I can _____   b. you'll do fine.

3. Try not to _____   c. bigger challenges than this.

4. I'm sure _____   d. worry about it.

2 Complete the conversation with the expressions from Exercise 1.

Lucia: Hey, Rick. How are you doing?

Rick: Not so good. I just fell off my skateboard.

Lucia: Oh, no. Do you need to have your knee checked?

Rick: No, it's just a small cut. I'm just worried about the skating competition tomorrow.

Lucia: 1_____
You're a great skater.

Rick: Not worry? That's impossible! You see, I haven't been skating well lately, so I'm not feeling confident at all.

Lucia: 2_____
You're probably falling because you're nervous.

Rick: Maybe. But I've worked so hard to achieve this goal, and now it seems impossible.

Lucia: Come on, Rick.
3_____
Remember the time you competed a few months after you had broken your arm?

Rick: Yeah. I did pretty well in that competition. But for some reason, I wasn't nervous like I am now.

Lucia: 4_____

Rick: Really? How?

Lucia: We'll skate together. We'll pretend it's the competition. Every time you fall, just get up again. We can practice all day if you want to. Before long, I don't think you'll be so nervous.

Rick: OK. You're right. I should keep trying. I won't give up!

1 Complete the sentences with the correct words.

achieve	addition	determined	help

1. I'll need _____ from my mother.

2. In _____, I will check online to see what activities are happening in my neighborhood.

3. I am _____ to do everything by myself.

4. In order to _____ this, I will take a class about web design.

2 Complete the text with the sentences from Exercise 1.

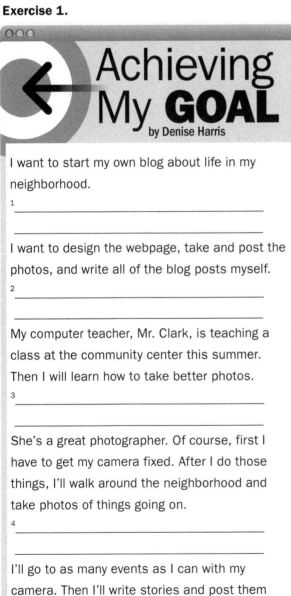

Achieving My GOAL
by Denise Harris

I want to start my own blog about life in my neighborhood.

1 _____

_____

I want to design the webpage, take and post the photos, and write all of the blog posts myself.

2 _____

_____

My computer teacher, Mr. Clark, is teaching a class at the community center this summer. Then I will learn how to take better photos.

3 _____

_____

She's a great photographer. Of course, first I have to get my camera fixed. After I do those things, I'll walk around the neighborhood and take photos of things going on.

4 _____

_____

I'll go to as many events as I can with my camera. Then I'll write stories and post them on my blog with my pictures.

3 Read the text again. Answer the questions.

1. What is Denise's goal?

_____

_____

2. What steps will Denise take to achieve her goal?

☑ learn about web design

❑ take a photography class

❑ have her computer fixed

❑ have her camera fixed

❑ learn to take better photos

❑ learn to write better in English

❑ take photos of activities in her neighborhood

❑ take photos of her life at home

❑ find out about activities from her mother

❑ find out about activities online

3. Look at the steps you checked in question 2. Which ones will Denise get help from other people to do?

_____

_____

_____

_____

_____

_____

1 Circle the correct words.

1. Jana **told** / **announced** me she was nervous about her test.

2. Bob **whispered** / **shouted** loudly at the game. He was thrilled to see his brother play basketball.

3. Luis **explained** / **reminded** that he was disappointed his team lost the soccer game.

4. Jun **complained** / **said** that he was a confident speaker, so I'm sure he was calm before he gave his speech.

5. Tina **suggested** / **reminded** us that we should be prepared for the storm.

6. I was miserable about having to clean the house until Paulina **promised** / **said** to help me.

2 Write the sentences from Exercise 1 under the correct pictures.

1. *I was miserable about having to clean the house until* _____ .

2. _____

3. _____

4. _____

5. _____

6. _____

3 Cross out the word that doesn't belong to each category.

1. **Something you type:**
   an email   ~~a phone call~~
   a social network post   a blog post

2. **Something you do online:**
   video chat   send a text message
   join a forum   write a microblog post

3. **A good feeling:**
   excited   proud   miserable   satisfied

4. **A bad feeling:**
   disappointed   miserable
   nervous   confident

5. **Something people sometimes do loudly:**
   shout   announce   whisper   complain

4 Complete the text with the correct words.

✓ achieve	deal with	progress
challenge	face	reward
commitments	goals	skills

Ways to ¹ *Achieve* Success

- ² _____ yourself every day. Then work hard to make ³ _____ so that you can reach your ⁴ _____ .

- Learn new ⁵ _____ . Teach yourself or take a class to learn something new.

- Keep the ⁶ _____ you make. It's important to do the things you say you'll do.

- ⁷ _____ problems quickly. The longer you wait to fix a problem, the harder it is to ⁸ _____ .

- Don't expect to get a ⁹ _____ for everything you do. Sometimes it's enough just to be successful.

5 Write the numbered sentences in the blog as reported speech.

○ ○ ○

Franco's Blog

Today's post: The future!

Hello, friends. ¹What will you do in the future? ²Goals are important. I want to know what your goals are! ³How are you going to reach them?

Lori: ⁴I want to be a computer programmer. ⁵I'm taking computer classes at school.

Aamir: ⁶I've played soccer for 10 years. ⁷Can you guess my future career?

Kwan: ⁸I went to Mexico on vacation. ⁹I want to improve my Spanish!

---

1. Franco *asked what we would do in the future* .

2. He said that _____ .

3. He _____ .

4. Lori _____ .

5. She _____ .

6. Aamir _____ .

7. He _____ .

8. Kwan _____ .

9. She _____ .

6 Complete the sentences with the correct reflexive pronouns.

1. Takeko sang by _____*herself*_____ at her last music performance.

2. I'm very proud that I achieved many of my goals by _____ .

3. Mindy, you shouldn't be disappointed in _____ . You did your best.

4. Josh announced that he would teach _____ to speak Chinese.

5. We promised _____ that we would take a vacation next year.

6. Tim and Carla prepared _____ for a difficult task.

7 Write sentences with causative *have/get*. Use the simple past.

1. we / get / our hair / cut

   We got our hair cut.

2. Lucia / have / her bike / fix

   _____

3. I / get / my arm / examine

   _____

4. Matt and Lynn / have / their house / paint

   _____

5. Chuck / get / his photo / take

   _____

8 Circle the correct words.

Yin: Hi, Eva. Are you ready for the music performance?

Eva: No, I'm not. I'm so nervous!

Yin: Try not to ¹**deal with / worry about** it. I'm sure you'll do ²**fine / proud**.

Eva: Well, I've practiced a lot, but I just don't want to go first. ³**Chatting with / According to** my sister, Hank Patterson went first last year, and he was so nervous that he couldn't play.

Yin: That's not what I ⁴**heard / happened**.

Eva: Really?

Yin: Yeah. I asked Hank what ⁵**had faced / had happened**, and he said that the audio system wasn't working.

Eva: I see. So, what did he do?

Yin: Well, Hank ⁶**said / told** that he didn't realize it at first. So he just played, but no one could hear him. They fixed the system, and he started again. Everything was fine.

Eva: I hope that doesn't happen to me. Now I'm really nervous.

Yin: Don't be! You've faced bigger ⁷**ideas / challenges** than this. You're going to be great!

The LONG WINTER

BEFORE YOU WATCH

1 Look at the pictures from the video. Do you think the sentences are true (T) or false (F)?

1. These people live in a big city.   _____

2. They spend most of their time outdoors.   _____

3. They grow their own vegetables.   _____

4. They fish in the winter.   _____

WHILE YOU WATCH

2 Watch the video. Circle the correct words.

1. In Alaska, it is cold for **three / eight** months of the year.

2. The Kilcher family uses **wood / oil** to heat their home.

3. They put their **food / clothes** in storage.

4. In the winter, they **can / can't** go to a supermarket for food.

5. Atz takes traps for **rabbits / bears** into the forest.

3 Watch the video again. Complete the sentences with the correct words.

builds	catch	cut down	goes	plan

1. The Kilchers _____ trees in the summer.

2. They _____ fish in the lake.

3. They _____ their meals for the months ahead.

4. Atz _____ a fire on the lake.

5. He _____ home with a bag of rabbits.

AFTER YOU WATCH

4 Work with a partner. Discuss: Which do you prefer, cold weather or hot weather? What do you like to do outdoors in cold weather? In hot weather?

> I prefer cold weather. I like skiing and ice skating in cold weather. I love swimming in hot weather.

An ISLAND FLOOD

BEFORE YOU WATCH

1 **Look at the pictures from the video. Then match the pictures to the sentences.**

a. 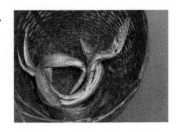   b.    c.

1. These are rice fields on the island of Bali in India. _____

2. People here eat a lot of fish. _____

3. These men are fishermen – they catch fish in the sea. _____

WHILE YOU WATCH

2 **Watch the video. Circle the correct words.**

1. Life isn't **nice / easy** here.

2. People depend on a few **fish / rice** fields.

3. Years ago, a **flood / storm** destroyed homes.

4. The men knew they needed to **buy / build** a wall.

5. They worked for **three / five** hours.

3 **Watch the video again. Match the phrases to make true sentences.**

1. At last, _____   a. water flooded the village.

2. During the night, _____   b. he went fishing.

3. Last week, _____   c. the men went home.

4. Years ago, _____   d. the men watched the waters rising.

AFTER YOU WATCH

4 **Work with a partner. Describe an extreme weather event in your life. What were you doing when it happened?**

> Last summer, there was a big storm. There was thunder and lightning and a lot of rain. I was playing soccer. We ran into the school and closed all the windows.

Get UP and GO!

BEFORE YOU WATCH

1 Look at the pictures from the video. Circle the correct words.

1. This special bed can wake you **up / down** in the morning.

2. It can also pull **off / in** your pajamas.

3. They purée the cereal **in / on** a blender for breakfast.

WHILE YOU WATCH

2 Watch the video. Check (✓) what the machine can do.

1. ❑ wake you

2. ❑ undress you

3. ❑ make breakfast

4. ❑ shower you

5. ❑ brush your hair

3 Watch the video again. Circle the correct answers.

1. A lot of people say they hate _____.
   a. going to bed   b. waking up   c. getting dressed

2. The machine _____ to wake you up.
   a. shakes you   b. plays music   c. showers you

3. First, they try giving the man some _____.
   a. milk   b. water   c. oatmeal

4. The man _____ the breakfast cereal.
   a. likes   b. loves   c. hates

5. What does the machine give the man at the end?
   a. shoes and socks   b. T-shirt and shorts   c. coat and hat

AFTER YOU WATCH

4 Work with a partner. Describe the differences between your morning routine during the week and on weekends. What do you do, and when?

> During the week, I get up at 6:30. I take a shower and brush my teeth. Then I get dressed. I eat breakfast around 7:00. On weekends, I usually sleep until 9. I wash my face, and then I eat breakfast. Then I get dressed around 10.

Irish DANCING

BEFORE YOU WATCH

1 Look at the pictures from the video. Do you think the sentences are true (*T*) or false (*F*)?

In Irish dancing, you have to:

1. wear sneakers _____

2. kick your legs high _____

3. hold your hands in the air _____

4. wear socks _____

WHILE YOU WATCH

2 Watch the video. Circle the correct answers.

1. What does the teacher say to the dancers?

   a. Hurry up!   b. Get up!   c. Pick it up!

2. This is Julia's _____ time at the World Championship.

   a. first   b. third   c. fourth

3. Julia won the World Championship _____ years ago.

   a. one   b. two   c. three

4. This year the Championship is in _____.

   a. Belfast   b. London   c. New York City

5. Julia wins _____ place.

   a. first   b. third   c. fourth

3 Watch the video again. Number the sentences 1–5 in the order that you hear them.

1. We're on the plane right now. _____

2. She dances tall and straight. _____

3. I am twelve years old. _____

4. Come on! Push it! _____

5. I'm Julia's mom. _____

AFTER YOU WATCH

4 Work with a partner. Do you or your classmates participate in any competitions? How do you prepare for them?

> I'm on the soccer team. We have a game every Saturday. We have to practice three times a week. We have to go to bed early the night before the game and eat a good breakfast in the morning!

Original *ART*

BEFORE YOU WATCH

1 Look at the pictures from the video. Complete the sentences with the correct words.

changed   face   painting

The Aborigines of Australia have an ancient tradition of _____. Their art is full of symbols

and patterns that have not _____ in thousands of years. The dots on this girl's _____

represent rainfall.

WHILE YOU WATCH

2 Watch the video. Are the sentences true (*T*) or false (*F*)? Correct the false sentences.

1. The Aborigines have lived in Australia for 4,000 years. _____

2. The land is very important to the Aborigines. _____

3. Some paintings show where stores are. _____

4. Many symbols in their art have changed. _____

5. Aboriginal body paintings use symbols, too. _____

3 Watch the video again. Check (✔) the sentences you hear.

1. ❑ Australia is an interesting place.

2. ❑ These paintings communicate essential information about the people.

3. ❑ Our whole land is ancient.

4. ❑ Some of these paintings are survival maps.

5. ❑ Everything tells a story.

AFTER YOU WATCH

4 Work with a partner. Make a list of the symbols you see every day. What do they communicate?

I see the recycling symbol on the bins at school. It means you can put your papers there instead of in the garbage.

A WORLD of MUSIC

BEFORE YOU WATCH

1 **Look at the pictures from the video. Then match the pictures to the sentences.**

a.    b.    c.

1. Indian music uses the **tabla**, a kind of drum, and the **sitar**, a stringed instrument. _____

2. An Aborigine in Australia plays the **didgeridoo**. _____

3. **Trumpets** are an important part of the Mexican mariachi sound. _____

WHILE YOU WATCH

2 **Watch the video. Circle the correct answers.**

1. Mariachi music has been around for _____ of years.
   a. hundreds   b. thousands   c. millions
2. The Spanish brought instruments like _____ to Mexico.
   a. sitars   b. tablas   c. guitars
3. The sitar is an _____ instrument.
   a. expensive   b. ancient   c. English
4. British musicians became interested in Indian music in the _____.
   a. 1950s   b. 1960s   c. 1970s
5. The didgeridoo is a _____ instrument.
   a. wood   b. stringed   c. wind
6. Aborigines have played didgeridoos for at least _____ years.
   a. 200   b. 2,000   c. 2,200

3 **Watch the video again. Match the nouns and adjectives.**

1. _____ mariachi music   a. strange
2. _____ the sitar and tabla   b. famous
3. _____ kangaroo and koala   c. lively
4. _____ didgeridoo   d. unusual

AFTER YOU WATCH

4 **Work in small groups. Discuss musicians from other countries: Who do you like? Describe their music.**

> I really like Lorde. She's from New Zealand. Her music is part pop, rock, and hip hop.

The AGE of DISCOVERY

BEFORE YOU WATCH

1 Look at the picture from the video. Complete the sentences with the correct words.

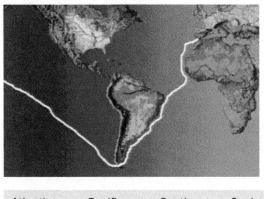

Atlantic	Pacific	South	Spain

In 1519, the famous explorer Ferdinand Magellan sailed from _____ across the _____ Ocean. He went around the bottom of _____ America, then crossed the _____ Ocean.

WHILE YOU WATCH

2 Watch the video. Number the events 1–5 in the order they occurred.

1. Magellan sails around South America. _____

2. One of Magellan's ships completes the journey. _____

3. Christopher Columbus discovers the Americas. _____

4. Magellan lives in a castle with the king and queen of Portugal. _____

5. Vasco de Gama sails around Africa to India. _____

3 Watch the video again. Complete the sentences with the correct places.

Asia	Philippines	Portugal	Strait of Magellan	Spain

1. Magellan was born in 1480 in _____.

2. Christopher Columbus was looking for _____ in 1492.

3. The king of _____ gave Magellan five boats.

4. The ocean waters in the _____ were very dangerous.

5. Magellan was killed in the _____.

AFTER YOU WATCH

4 Work in small groups. Take turns naming exciting activities you have done and activities you want to do.

> I've gone rafting. I really want to go scuba diving.

Fun in AUSTRALIA

BEFORE YOU WATCH

1 Look at the pictures from the video. Complete the sentences with the correct words.

camels   sheep   toads

Australia has many different kinds of animals and some very unusual sports. _____ are not easy

to ride, but Australians race them. They also have contests to see who can cut a _____'s wool the

fastest. In some parts of the country, people paint numbers on these small _____ and race them!

WHILE YOU WATCH

2 Watch the video. Complete the sentences with the correct words.

1. Uluru is a giant _____.

2. Australia has nearly a million wild _____.

3. The cane _____ is poisonous.

4. _____ shearing is a big sport in Australia.

5. Australian rules _____ is the country's favorite sport.

3 Watch the video again. Number the things 1–5 in the order you see them.

1. kangaroos   _____

2. sheep   _____

3. Sydney Opera House _____

4. camels   _____

5. toads   _____

AFTER YOU WATCH

4 Work with a partner. What are some other contests with animals in the world? Make a list, then share it with another pair.

Country	Animal	Contest
Ireland, Scotland, England	*dogs*	*sheep herding*

Creepy CREATURES

BEFORE YOU WATCH

1 Look at the picture from the video and read the sentences. Match the words and the definitions.

1. _____ capture
2. _____ phobia
3. _____ serpent

a. snake
b. catch
c. extreme fear

4. Do you have any phobias? Explain.

_____

_____

_____

_____

This man is <u>capturing</u> a King Cobra. Many people have a <u>phobia</u> of this <u>serpent</u>.

WHILE YOU WATCH

2 Watch the video. Are the sentences true (*T*) or false (*F*)? Correct the false sentences.

1. The video shows more than eight different kinds of snakes. _____

2. The snake around Jeff Corwin's arm scares him. _____

3. Some King Cobras live near rivers. _____

4. Jeff's friend has never seen a King Cobra before. _____

5. To catch a King Cobra, you must hold its head. _____

3 Watch the video again. Check (✓) the words you hear to describe the King Cobra.

1. ❑ nervous
2. ❑ king of the serpents
3. ❑ snake-eater
4. ❑ terrified
5. ❑ awesome

AFTER YOU WATCH

4 Work in small groups. Make a list of three to four animals that terrify people. Why do you think people are afraid of these animals? Share your list with other groups.

1. *lions: They can attack people.*
2. *snakes: A snake bite can be poisonous.*
3. *sharks: A shark might attack you when you're swimming in the ocean.*

Calendars of the
ANCIENT MAYA

BEFORE YOU WATCH

1 Look at the pictures from the video. Circle the correct answers.

This calendar **use / was used** by the ancient Mayan civilization in Mexico and Central America.
Each day **had / has had** a name and a symbol. The Maya **predicted / have predicted** good days
and bad days.

2 Look at the Cimi symbol in the Mayan calendar. What do you think it means?

_____

_____

_____

WHILE YOU WATCH

3 Watch the video. Circle the correct answers.

1. The Mayan calendar showed each **day / week** of the year.

2. The Maya planted on **sunny / good** days.

3. The solar calendar had **18 / 20** months.

4. There were **five / six** bad days in a year.

5. The temple of Kukulkan has **360 / 365** steps.

4 Watch the video again. Match the phrases to make true sentences.

1. The Maya _____

2. Each day _____

3. Imix _____

4. Cimi _____

5. Nothing important _____

a. had a symbol.

b. was a good day.

c. watched the sun and moon.

d. happened on bad days.

e. was a bad day.

AFTER YOU WATCH

**5 Work with a partner. Make a calendar for the next week. Use symbols to indicate good days and bad days.
Say one good thing that will happen to your partner on the good days, and one bad thing that will happen on
the bad days.**

Next Monday will be a bad day. You will lose your backpack. Next
Tuesday will be a good day. You will win tickets to a concert.

Working TOGETHER

BEFORE YOU WATCH

1 Look at the pictures from the video. Complete the sentences with the correct words.

business	field	plant	together	vote	weather

1. The prickly pear is a type of _____ that likes hot _____.

2. These women are working _____ in a _____ in Mexico.

3. The women _____ on how to run their _____.

WHILE YOU WATCH

2 Watch the video. Number the events 1–5 in order.

1. The women started a business. _____

2. The cooperative sells products in the US and Mexico. _____

3. Many men moved away. _____

4. Most people worked in the fields. _____

5. The women voted on how to do things. _____

3 Watch the video again. Circle the correct answers.

1. What did most farms in Ayoquesco grow before 1979?

   a. prickly pear   b. tobacco   c. cactus plants

2. What happened in 1979?

   a. The factory closed.   b. The women earned money.   c. The farms failed.

3. Mexicans add prickly pear to _____.

   a. salads   b. soups   c. both a. and b.

4. In a cooperative, _____ runs the business.

   a. one person   b. a small group   c. everyone

5. In the sentence "A man from the government regularly comes to inspect their factory," to *inspect* means to _____.

   a. photograph   b. examine   c. visit

AFTER YOU WATCH

4 Work with a small group. Imagine that you're going to start a business. Discuss and vote on these questions:

1. What kind of business will it be?

2. Where will it be located?

3. How many people are going to work there?

> We're going to start a restaurant. It will be next to the gym. About 12 people will work there.

Watch Your IDENTITY

BEFORE YOU WATCH

1 Do you spend a lot of time online? Answer the questions.

1. What personal information do you share online?

_____

_____

2. What information should you not share?

_____

_____

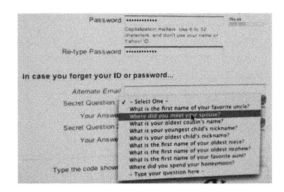

WHILE YOU WATCH

2 Watch the video. Number the sentences 1–5 in the order you hear them.

1. Sometimes you'll get a message from someone you don't know. _____

2. A criminal just needs your name and some numbers. _____

3. You just have to be aware of who you're adding as a friend. _____

4. Social media is a great way to connect with friends. _____

5. The site will ask for your name. _____

3 Watch the video again. Check (✓) the sentences you hear.

1. ❑ People spend a lot of time online during the day.

2. ❑ Criminals use social media sites, too.

3. ❑ It tells you to go to a website.

4. ❑ They can use that information to get credit cards.

5. ❑ Delete these emails if you get them.

AFTER YOU WATCH

4 Work with a partner. Discuss: What would you do if you discovered that one of your online friends was a fake?

> If I found out one of my friends online was a fake, I'd email him to ask who he was.

> I would delete his or her contact information from all of my social media sites.

Where Does It ALL GO?

BEFORE YOU WATCH

1 Look at the picture from the video. Answer the questions.

What materials do you think this trash is made of?
If we throw trash on the ground, where does it go?

_____

_____

_____

_____

WHILE YOU WATCH

2 Watch the video. Match the events and the places.

1. The North Pacific Gyre is in _____.

2. There is enough plastic in the gyre to cover _____.

3. The toys fell into the sea just north of _____.

4. In 1995, some of the toys wound up in _____.

5. Between 1996 and 2000, many of the toys worked their way into _____.

6. In 2007, a few of the rubber duckies washed up in _____.

a. the Atlantic Ocean

b. Hawaii

c. South America

d. Britain

e. the Pacific Ocean

f. Texas

3 Watch the video again. Complete the sentences with the numbers you hear.

| ¼ (a quarter)   29   71   139 |

1. Oceans cover _____ million square miles of Earth.

2. Water covers _____ percent of the planet.

3. People throw nearly _____ of a million kilos of garbage into the sea every day.

4. A shipment of _____ thousand toys fell into the sea.

AFTER YOU WATCH

4 How much garbage do you produce in a day? Complete the chart, listing everything you threw away yesterday. Share your list with a partner.

#	Item	Material	Where did you throw item(s) away?
2	bottles	plastic	recycling bin

Build IT BETTER

BEFORE YOU WATCH

1 Look at the pictures from the video. Complete the sentences with the correct words.

| energy | heated | roof | solar | tubes |

1. _____ from the sun is absorbed by these _____ panels.

2. The _____ on the _____ of this building contain water. The water is _____ by the sun.

WHILE YOU WATCH

2 Watch the video. Are the sentences true (*T*) or false (*F*)? Correct the false sentences.

1. There was a tornado in the town in 2007.   _____

2. The tornado destroyed 90 percent of the homes and businesses.   _____

3. The reflectors always face north.   _____

4. The solar panels turn sunlight into heat.   _____

5. The solar panels can power the whole building.   _____

3 Watch the video again. Circle the correct words.

1. The town was **hit / reduced** by a huge tornado.

2. It was **suggested / decided** to use solar energy.

3. How were the solar tubes **placed / put** in the roof?

4. First, holes were **drilled / made**.

5. Solar panels were **built / rebuilt**.

AFTER YOU WATCH

4 Work in small groups. Discuss what people in your community do to help the environment.

> Most people recycle their bottles and trash. There's a big garden downtown. People plant vegetables and flowers there.

Land of VOLCANOES

BEFORE YOU WATCH

1 Look at the picture from the video. Complete the text with the correct words.

| active | cloud | damage | erupt | eruption | warn |

_____ volcanoes can _____ at any time. They produce a _____ of rock and ash. They can kill people and _____ airplanes. Some scientists study these volcanoes and _____ people when there is an _____.

WHILE YOU WATCH

2 Watch the video. Answer the questions yes (Y) or no (N).

1. Is the region with volcanoes close to Moscow?   _____

2. Does Sasha study active volcanoes?   _____

3. Can the warning save thousands of airlines?   _____

4. Did the volcano erupt a few weeks ago?   _____

5. Did small eruptions continue for weeks?   _____

3 Watch the video again. Match the phrases to make true sentences.

1. Sasha has visited _____   a. activity in one of the volcanoes.

2. Sasha has taken _____   b. the airlines.

3. Their warnings can save _____   c. the volcanoes many times.

4. The seismograph had shown _____   d. regular samples from the volcanoes.

5. Sasha and his team had to warn _____   e. people's lives.

AFTER YOU WATCH

4 Work in small groups. Discuss: What natural disasters have occurred in the world in the past year? What happened?

> Last year, there was a big flood in Germany. It rained for four days. People had to leave their houses.

Storm CHASERS

BEFORE YOU WATCH

1 Look at the pictures from the video. Answer the questions.

1. What do you think the men are watching? Where do you think they are?

_____

_____

2. What natural disasters can cause this kind of damage?

_____

_____

WHILE YOU WATCH

2 Watch the video. Circle the correct answers.

1. Dixie Alley is in the _____ of the United States.

   a. north   b. south   c. west

2. The Storm Chasers are _____.

   a. teachers   b. police   c. scientists

3. _____ tornadoes are very violent.

   a. F5   b. F15   c. F50

4. The Storm Chasers try to _____ people.

   a. warn   b. talk to   c. educate

3 Watch the video again. Complete the sentences with the correct numbers.

60	130	180	321	400

1. Every year, tornadoes kill about _____ people.

2. F5 tornadoes have winds higher than _____ kilometers per hour.

3. The F5 stayed on the ground for _____ kilometers.

4. There were over _____ tornadoes in Dixie Alley that day.

5. Unfortunately, _____ people died in the storm.

AFTER YOU WATCH

4 Work in small groups. Discuss: How do people get warnings about extreme weather? What do you think is the best way?

> A lot of people listen to the radio. I also check the weather on the Internet.

Social NETWORKS

BEFORE YOU WATCH

1 Answer the questions.

1. What Internet sites do you visit most often?

_____

2. Name two to three popular social media sites.

_____

_____

_____

3. What does the number of online "friends"
   or "followers" someone has tell you?

_____

_____

WHILE YOU WATCH

2 Watch the video. Circle the correct answers.

1. The narrator says that _____ changed the way people thought about video.

   a. Facebook   b. YouTube   c. Wikipedia

2. Mark Zuckerberg believes that _____ made Facebook so popular.

   a. college students   b. high school students   c. relationships

3. Zuckerberg explains that the *social graph* is a map of connections between _____.

   a. places   b. people   c. websites

4. Jimmy Wales says that communities can produce _____ of very high quality.

   a. work   b. writing   c. ideas

5. All three men believe that _____ are important.

   a. schools   b. companies   c. communities

3 Watch the video again. Check (✓) the sentences you hear.

1. ❏ Now, anyone with a video can be famous.

2. ❏ The Internet's about connecting individuals.

3. ❏ And, I mean, there are billions of them across the country.

4. ❏ New relationships mean new users.

5. ❏ Wikipedia is now the world's most popular encyclopedia.

AFTER YOU WATCH

**4 Work in small groups. Discuss: What social media sites are the best for staying in touch with friends?
For sharing photos? For messaging?**

> Facebook's OK for staying in touch. I use Instagram for
> photos, and I use my phone for messaging.

The LANGUAGE of the FUTURE?

BEFORE YOU WATCH

1 Look at the pictures from the video. Answer the questions.

1. What language or languages do people speak in China?

_____

2. What are some things China produces?

_____

_____

WHILE YOU WATCH

2 Watch the video. Are the sentences true (*T*) or false (*F*)? Correct the false sentences.

1. About four billion people live in China. _____

2. China has the strongest economy in the world. _____

3. Mandarin has over 40,000 written characters. _____

4. The Chinese developed a system that uses the Roman alphabet. _____

5. The narrator asks if Mandarin is the world's number one language now. _____

3 Watch the video again. Complete the sentences with the words you hear.

1. Everything in China is _____.

2. The country already produces many things, like the _____ you're wearing.

3. But everyone can understand one _____ language: Mandarin.

4. In the late _____, the Chinese developed a system called "Pinyin."

5. There are Chinese people who speak _____ all over the world.

AFTER YOU WATCH

4 Work with a partner. Make a list of things you own or use that are made in China. Do you think your children will speak Mandarin?

1. backpack

2. sneakers

3. cell phone

4. computer

LIFEGUARD *and* ATHLETE

BEFORE YOU WATCH

1 Look at the pictures from the video. Complete the sentences with the correct words.

| cool off | lifeguard | rescue | surfboard |

1. On hot days, people go to this beach in Australia to _____.

2. This woman is a _____. She uses her _____ to _____ people from the dangerous waters.

WHILE YOU WATCH

2 Watch the video. Answer the questions about Candice.

1. How many people has Candice rescued?   _____

2. What was her goal when she was 12?   _____

3. What does she say she could not survive without?   _____

4. What is her goal in the Lifesaving Championship?   _____

5. How does she feel about her performance in the first race?   _____

3 Watch the video again. Circle the correct words.

1. Every year, dangerous waters **take / save** the lives of people.

2. If a rescue situation **comes up / goes off**, Candice is the first one out there.

3. Sometimes she must bring people she rescues **out to shore / back to life**.

4. She must put her fears of the ocean **out of her mind / on the table**.

5. The first race is usually her worst because it takes her a bit to **cool off / warm up**.

AFTER YOU WATCH

4 Work with a partner. What are some other life-saving jobs?

> Well, the police save people's lives, and doctors and nurses do, too.

Circus STAR

BEFORE YOU WATCH

1 Look at the pictures from the video. Do you think the sentences are true (T) or false (F)?

1. In Russia, the circus is considered an art, like ballet or theater. _____

2. The Russian government owns some of the circuses in Russia. _____

3. Most circus acrobats perform with wild animals. _____

4. Many Russians think that being a circus performer is an excellent job. _____

WHILE YOU WATCH

2 Watch the video. Are the sentences true (T) or false (F)? Correct the false sentences.

1. Aliona dreams of being a circus director. _____

2. Aliona's last practice doesn't go very well. _____

3. She is performing for the top athletes in Russia's circuses. _____

4. She earns her circus diploma. _____

5. She decides to take her dream job in Moscow. _____

3 Watch the video again. Answer the questions about Aliona.

1. What must Aliona do in four weeks? _____

2. What happens during her last practice? _____

3. What is she offered after her performance? _____

4. What does she decide to do? _____

AFTER YOU WATCH

4 Work with a partner. Discuss: What was a goal you accomplished when you were very young? What challenges did you face?

> I really wanted to learn how to ride a bike. At first, I fell a lot, and I was a little scared of hurting myself. But now, I ride my bike everywhere!

Notes